Louis Bourdaloue

The Spiritual Retreat of Father Bourdaloue Adapted to the Use of Pastors of Souls

Louis Bourdaloue

The Spiritual Retreat of Father Bourdaloue Adapted to the Use of Pastors of Souls

ISBN/EAN: 9783744659529

Printed in Europe, USA, Canada, Australia, Japan

Cover: Foto ©Lupo / pixelio.de

More available books at **www.hansebooks.com**

THE SPIRITUAL RETREAT

OF

FATHER BOURDALOUE, S.J.

ADAPTED TO THE USE

OF

PASTORS OF SOULS.

Be renewed in the spirit of your mind, and put on the new man.—EPH. iv., 23.

LEAMINGTON:
ART AND BOOK COMPANY, BEDFORD STREET.
LONDON:
BURNS AND OATES, ORCHARD ST. AND PATERNOSTER ROW.
NEW YORK:
CATHOLIC PUBLICATION SOCIETY COMPANY,
1885.

THE SPIRITUAL RETREAT, &c.

MEDITATION FOR THE EVE OF A RETREAT.

I will lead her (Israel) into the wilderness, and will speak to her heart.—OSEE ii.

FIRST POINT.—God has inspired me with the desire and intention of making this Retreat. The resolution, which I have formed to withdraw myself for a few days from my usual intercourse with the world and go into solitude, proceeds undoubtedly from a motion of divine grace. I ought, therefore, to correspond with this heavenly call by endeavouring to perform all the exercises of the Retreat, which I am commencing, with a view to a thorough conversion and amendment of my life.

To be called to a Retreat is a grace of predilection not granted to all. Thousands of worldlings are living in the servitude of sin, and many even of my own state in the omission of important duties, and who yet never think of having recourse to a Retreat as the sovereign remedy for their spiritual disorders. Since God, therefore, by this call has shewn a singular mercy to me, I ought to correspond with it in the most earnest and perfect manner possible.

The Retreat, on which I am now entering, is perhaps the last that I shall ever have the opportunity of making. Were I certain that it is so, with what fervour should I perform it? If, then, I have hitherto wholly neglected this important means of salvation, or, if my former Retreats have been productive of but little amendment in me, I must try, now at least, to compensate for past omissions —to repair whatever has been defective— and to perfect in my soul the work of God.

SECOND POINT.—The Almighty, in his desire to sanctify me, calls me to interior, much more than to exterior solitude. Hence, during these holy days, it is my duty to banish from my mind and heart whatever may divert my attention from God. I should try to spend these days as though there were not in the world another being besides God and myself, so that I may be able truly to say with the spouse in the Canticles: *my beloved to me, and I to my beloved.*—(Can. ii.) Far, then, from my mind be every thought foreign to the great work which I have taken in hand. These few days belong so entirely to God and my own soul, that, until their conclusion,

I have no business to think, even for one moment, on any worldly care, or to be solicitous about my ordinary duties. The Almighty wishes to be alone with me, that he may speak to my heart; but, if he finds it pre-engaged by any passion, or under the influence of uneasiness or any earthly attachment, he will neither speak to me, nor shall I be in the disposition to listen to him.

Woe, then, to me, if I bring into the sanctuary of holy solitude a dissipated mind. Woe to me, if I render myself unfit for keeping up a communication with my divine spouse, by entertaining any irregular desire or yielding to any human attachment. As God is going to speak to my heart, I ought to be disposed to say to him with all the sincerity of David: *I will hear what the Lord God has to say to me;* (Psalm lxxxiv.) or with Samuel: *Speak, Lord, for thy servant heareth* (1 Kings, iii.) Like his blessed mother, I ought to. be prepared to treasure up in my heart every word that he may be pleased to speak to me.

THIRD POINT.—The end of my Retreat must not merely be to taste the delights of holy solitude, nor even to spend more time than usual in prayer or other religious exercises. These are, indeed, essential accompaniments of, but do not constitute, a good Retreat. My object must be, to discover the real dispositions of my heart—to see clearly my imperfections and evil habits—to acquire a thorough knowledge of the designs of God in my regard—to examine the manner in which I perform all my duties—to renew the spirit of my vocation—to amend my life—in a word, to become what St. Paul calls *a new creature in Jesus Christ.*—(2 Cor.: v.) If my Retreat do not terminate in this result, and I leave it without having both discovered and corrected my ordinary failings, any sentiments of devotion, however tender and affectionate, that I may have conceived, can be regarded as nothing better than pure illusions. Neither must my design be directed to vague and general objects. To render it completely effective, I must aim at something specific and determinate, and with this view, I must examine narrowly in what particular duties to God, to myself, and to my neighbour, I am deficient, and direct my Retreat to the repairing of these deficiencies.

CONCLUDING PRAYER.—Enlighten, O God, my understanding, that I may distinctly discover my sins and imperfections, and grant me grace to apply to them the necessary remedies. Since thou hast called me into this solitude, make known to me now the perfection to which I ought to aspire, and the means whereby it is to be attained. Let not what to numbers of sinners has been the means of their conversion, become, through sloth or neglect on my part, the subject of my greater condemnation.

O God, what wilt thou have me to do? Do thou prescribe the work which I ought to perform during these days of salvation, and I, with the assistance of thy grace, will remove every obstacle to the accomplishment of thy adorable designs. I seem to feel in my heart that happy disposition, which enables me to use with humble confidence the words of thy holy prophet: *my heart is ready, O God, my heart is ready.*—(Ps. lvi.) Should the subtleties of self-love herein deceive me, help me, O Lord, to discover and overcome them. Purify this heart which, at least, feels a desire to obey thee, and has now retired from all intercourse with creatures, in order to receive more perfectly the impressions of thy holy grace and spirit.

First Day.

FIRST MEDITATION.

ON THE PERFECTION REQUIRED IN A PASTOR.

I have chosen you and appointed that you should go and bring forth fruit. . . . You are not of this world.—JOHN xv.

FIRST POINT.—As a creature of God, I am obliged to serve him: as a Christian, I am under the necessity of conforming to the sacred laws of the Gospel: and, as a priest and pastor of souls, I have contracted with the Almighty still more sacred obligations, whereby I am bound to the performance of particular duties tending to my own greater sanctification and the salvation of the souls of others. In calling me to the priesthood God had both these objects in view; but it is principally for the more complete accomplishment of the latter that he requires me to aim at a higher degree of virtue than other Christians. He wishes to propose me as a model to the world, that my conversation, my actions, and my entire life, may do honour to his service, edify my neighbour, and be a public and visible lesson of instruction and exhortation to all around me. He desires to set me up as a light to the world, and as a mirror, in which deluded worldlings may see the corruptions and errors of their practices and maxims. The special graces bestowed on me at my ordination had this perfection for their object, and it is only by a faithful correspondence with them that I can expect to share in the riches of God's glory.

For me, therefore, to aim at perfection and to attain salvation are things inseparable. To content myself with a common or imperfect degree of virtue would be a crime, the very thought of which ought to make me tremble. Then, what a reproach it should be to me, to know that any of my own flock are more desirous of perfection than myself, more earnest in their endeavours to arrive at it, and in reality more perfect! Have I not cause to blush, when I see any of them more mortified, more humble, and more charitable than myself? Oh! how awful is the thought of my having one day to stand before that judgment seat, where these examples will be adduced to confound my sloth and indifference! Besides, ought I not to tremble at the reflection, that, after having been so many years a priest, I have made so little progress in perfection, or perhaps have never thought seriously about it! It may be, that I am less perfect now, than when I entered the priesthood—that I am daily retrograding, instead of advancing, in the house of God. Is this doing what the Almighty requires of me? Is this fulfilling the end of my vocation?

SECOND POINT.—As a pastor of souls I am the minister of a crucified Master, and am obliged myself to be crucified and dead to the world. This spiritual crucifixion and death to the world consists in a total disengagement of my affections from it, and in the absolute renunciation of all human views, motives and pretensions. I must, therefore, live in the world as in a state of durance; the world must be my cross, as I ought most assuredly be a cross to it, by the opposition which should ever subsist between our respective sentiments, principles, and practices. If then, notwithstanding my sacred engagement ever to confront the world with the rules of the Gospel, I am still in love with it, and it with me;—if I am pleased with the generality of its ways, and it with mine;—if a mutual compromise has been entered into between us;—I renounce the character, and retain nothing but the name, of a priest. If, in a state which dedicates me in a singular manner to God, I employ myself with things that are not of God;—if, in a state in which I ought to hold frequent and intimate communications with God, I am disgusted with holy exercises and perform them with indifference;—if, instead of trying to keep my soul pure from the smallest stains, as becomes one ever employed about sacred things, I suffer it to be defiled with guilt, which either destroys or endangers the ground-work and essentials of the life of grace;—if, in short, instead of trying to grow rich for heaven, I do my works without any thing of the interior spirit, and mainly to please the world;— by all, or any part of, such conduct I pervert my vocation from its true end, I disgrace the sacred name which I bear and my ministry is vain. It is but too true, that such pastors are to be found; and am I not of the number of them?

THIRD POINT.—The sanctity of the sacerdotal character implies, also, the obligation of dying to myself. The exterior world, indeed, which I am bound to renounce, is not half so dangerous to me, nor so much opposed to my advancement in perfection, as those powerful enemies, which I always carry about me, and which enter into the very composition of my nature, *the concupiscence of the flesh, the concupiscence of the eyes, and the pride of life.*—(1 John ii.)— These enemies will never suffer me to be at ease, but one or the other of them will always keep me in action: and so important is success to me in this warfare, that my progress in perfection is ever to be estimated by the victories which I gain over sensuality, covetousness and pride. If these inordinate inclinations influence me, they will operate as a poison and infect all that is virtuous in my performances; whereas, to hold them in subjection is the most unequivocal mark of solid virtue.

Sensible, therefore, of my danger, and aware that I am engaged in a warfare, which can terminate only with my life, I must ever be upon the watch against all the movements of my passions, lest they should take me by surprise, and, in an unguarded moment, gain the ascendancy over me. My only security is, to walk in the footsteps of Him, who has said, that he is *the way, the truth, and the life;* (John xiv.) and to *take up my cross and follow him daily*, (Luke ix.) by cheerfully enduring, and at the same time, esteeming and cherishing the austerities, labours, privations and humiliations of my ministry. This will keep me in the constant practice of the exterior mortification of my senses and of the interior denial of my will; and thus shall I truly die to myself.—All this is doubtless difficult, and requires great resolution and courage; but, can I reasonably expect that heaven is to cost me nothing? or shall I dare attempt to widen the path, which the Saviour of the world has declared to be narrow?

FIRST MEDITATION. 11

Would it not ill become one commissioned by Jesus Christ to be a leader of his soldiers under the standard of the cross, to lose courage and run away at the sight of the enemy?

CONCLUDING PRAYER.—O Lord, I have hitherto had but a very imperfect idea of the excellence of my vocation. But, being now made sensible of it, I am determined to begin from this day to esteem it as I ought, and to labour to acquire that true disengagement of affection from earthly things, and that crucifixion to the world and all my concupiscences, which constitute the perfection of the state to which thou hast called me, and which are so essentially requisite to make me a light and a model to those under my charge. The cause of my past misfortunes has been, that my desires were too weak and languid, merely momentary and transient; such *desires* as thou hast declared *kill the slothful, because his hands have refused to work at all.* (Prov. xxi.) Grant me, therefore, at this time, a fervent, efficacious and practical desire of perfection, such as will be followed and sustained by holy perseverance. To effect this, bring often to my mind the end of my vocation, the forgetfulness of which has, on numberless occasions, been so fatal to me.

I clearly forsee the obstacles which sloth and self-love will oppose to the observance of my present resolutions. I am sensible of the difficulties with which I shall have to contend, and of the sacrifices that I shall be required to make. But I know and acknowledge this day before heaven and earth, that they are sacrifices essential to the accomplishment of the end of my vocation and to the attainment of salvation. When, therefore, O Lord, my unhappy self-love prompts me to study my own ease and convenience to the predjudice of the duty which I owe to thee, call to my remembrance, I beseech thee, for what purpose I was made a priest. When I meet with trials, humiliations, and crosses, or when I feel either disrelish or disgust in the performance of my ordinary duties, remind me of the end for which I renounced the world, and chose thee for *the portion of my inheritance and my chalice.* These reflections, aided by the grace and unction of thy Holy Spirit, will give me courage and strength in the hour of trial, and will enable me to advance steadily in the path of perfection.

SECOND MEDITATION.

ON MORTAL SIN.

Know and see, what an evil it is to have forsaken the Lord thy God.—JEREM. vii.

FIRST POINT.—Mortal sin is not only the greatest of all evils, but, properly speaking, it is the only real evil in the world; for nothing but sin is an absolute evil. Sickness, poverty, contempt, and whatever else men are accustomed to regard as evils, are, in the designs of God, and, if properly borne, always become to us, real blessings. Of sin, as being a pure and essential evil, God neither is, nor can be, the author. As God is the sovereign good, so sin is the sovereign evil; and the same motives which oblige me to love the former with a sovereign love, indispensibly require me to detest the latter with a sovereign hatred. I must hate sin as much as I love God. If there be any created thing, which enjoys an equal share with God in my affections, I cannot be said to love him as I ought; and if I dread any other evil as much as, or more than, mortal sin, I cannot be said to fly and detest it as much as I am obliged.

But the most perfect idea that can be formed of mortal sin is, to consider it as the *sovereign evil of God*, as a formal contempt of Him, and a preference of some creature to Him. This preference consists in the sinner's choosing to forfeit the grace of God, when placed between the two alternatives of offending Him or of renouncing his own gratification. He knows God to be infinitely superior to all created things, and still he dares to offer Him the insult of giving the preference in his affections to some despicable creature.

A further estimate may be made of the malice of mortal sin from these four equally certain and terrible considerations:—1st. That for one only sin of pride, God hurled Lucifer and his companions (the most beautiful creatures that he had made) from heaven into the abyss of hell, and changed them into hideous devils; and, without allowing them time to repent, delivered them up to the eternal rigours of his justice. What an example is this, and how ought it to make me fear, lest He, who would not spare his angels after one sin, should be provoked by my repeated treasons against him, to close his mercy in my regard? 2d. That for one only sin of disobedience, God banished the first man out of paradise, deprived him of all the privileges of his state of innocence, and condemned him and all his posterity to death;—that, in punishment of this one sin, we are all born children of wrath, heirs to the calamities of this life and excluded from the kingdom of heaven. How awful is this vengeance of a God, who is equity itself, and infinitely just in all his judgments! 3d. That, to expiate this crime of disobedience, it was required that the Son of God should become incarnate and humble himself unto death, as nothing less than the humiliation and death of a God-Man would be received in reparation of the glory of the Deity, and as a compensation for the injury done to Him by sin. And 4th. That for one mortal sin, the mere act of a moment, God has prepared an eternity of torments, and that between sin and this eternal punishment there is no more than a just proportion.— These are truths founded upon divine faith; and if among Christians there be any who refuse to believe them, the reason is, that they know not the malice of mortal sin and the sovereign injury which it does to God.

SECOND POINT.—To comprehend the entire malice of mortal sin, it is necessary to consider it, also, as the *sovereign evil of man*, as depriving him of the friendship of God, breaking the bonds whereby God and man are united, and causing a total separation between them; robbing man of the life of grace, and bringing death to his soul. From these effects sin takes the name of *mortal.*

The grace enjoyed by man in the state of justice, is to him the principle of a supernatural life. The moment that he forfeits this grace, he becomes dead in the sight of God.

Impressed with a sense of these truths, can I be surprised at two others, not less incontrovertible than terrible? 1st. That mortal sin robs the soul of all the merit which it had acquired in the state of grace. Had I amassed immense treasures of merit—were I as holy as the apostles, by the commission of one mortal sin I lose all. This merit, it is true, will revive upon my repentance; but, should I die without being restored to grace, there will be no reward for my former good works. 2d. That actions the most holy and virtuous of themselves, when performed by a person in mortal sin, are of no avail towards a happy eternity. Whole days and years spent in prayer, the practice of the austerities of the anchorets, the observance of all the Christian precepts of piety and charity, my daily labour for the good of souls, all are dead works, so long as I myself am dead in mortal sin; and, whatever mercy God may hereafter show me, these works will never be crowned. O, what a state of poverty and wretchedness is that of mortal sin!

Have I never in my life been guilty of mortal sin? Am I not at this moment in that state? I cannot tell, because *I know not whether I am worthy of love or hatred.* (Eccle. ix.) Lost in this frightful abyss of uncertainty, all that I can do is, to build a holy confidence in the mercy of God on the foundation of a laborious and penitential life.

Third Point.—The sanctity of my state and the graces received at my ordination, are by no means an infallible preservative against mortal sin. Angels fell in heaven; the first man, notwithstanding the state of grace and innocence in which he was created, sinned in the earthly paradise; Judas became an apostate in the school of Jesus Christ; and many by their irregular and wicked lives have disgraced the sacred character of the priesthood. These dreadful misfortunes happen by the permission of the Almighty, who has his reasons for permitting them; but they ought to remind me of the admonition of the apostle: *Let him that stands, take heed lest he fall.* (1 Cor. x.)

I am, in many respects, more exposed to sin than the generality of Christians. The necessity of frequently celebrating the holy mysteries, and the many other sacred functions, which I may at any moment be called upon to perform, require that I should always keep myself in a state of grace. I am more exposed than a laic to the snares of pride, avarice, and other vices; and yet greater perfection is required from me than from him in the virtues to which these vices are opposed. Being set up by the Almighty to be a light to the world, men look to me for examples of every virtue, and a fault, which in one of the common faithful would be considered trivial, may in me be the source of grievous scandal.

It is, in fact, true to say, that, by reason of the sanctity of my state, a mortal sin committed by me is more heinous in the sight of God than the same sin committed by a layman. In many cases, what in the latter would be but a simple sin, would in me be attended with circumstances of great aggravation, and even be altered into a crime of sacrilege. Am I hence to conclude, that it would have been better for me not to have embraced my present state? God forbid. As well might I imagine that it had been better for me not to have been made a Christian, because the sins of a Christian are more heinous than those of a pagan. It would have been a crime in me not to have followed my vocation. He who called me to the Priesthood knew how to proportion his graces to my necessities. All that I have to do is, to beware of presumption, to trust neither to my state nor to myself, but to endeavour, as the Apostle recommends, to *work out my salvation with fear and trembling.* —(Philip: ii.)

CONCLUDING PRAYER.— Perfect, O God, by thy grace what thou hast begun by thy mercy. Suffer not the world to follow me into thy holy sanctuary: hold me securely in thy arms against the assaults of my enemies. Woe to me, if *in the land of Saints I commit iniquity.*—(Isaiah: xxvi.) I know not the secrets of my own heart; but thou, O Lord, knowest them. Does there lie concealed therein any secret poison, which infects my performances? Does any sin keep me at a distance from thee? Make known to me, O God, my real state; and, if there be aught amiss, I am determined to amend it during this Retreat. Whatever good I may have hitherto performed, and however fortunate I may have been in avoiding mortal sin, I will always fear my own weakness and constantly pray for thy grace to keep me in vigilance. By thy assistance I will have continual recourse to thee; I will be circumspect in my whole conduct, and will always try to forecast and avoid the most trifling danger of falling into the transgression of any of thy commandments.

THIRD MEDITATION.

ON VENIAL SIN.

Grieve not the Holy Spirit.—Eph. iv.

FIRST POINT —It is not unusual to make light of venial sin; but a thorough understanding of its nature and its consequences will make me judge quite otherwise concerning it, and induce me to use corresponding care to avoid it.

A sufficient motive to deter me from committing venial sin ought to be the knowledge that it is offensive to God. It does not, indeed, cause a total separation between God and me, but it occasions a coolness. By committing a venial sin I do not extinguish his Holy Spirit in me, but I grieve and afflict it. Hence, as being offensive to God, I ought to dread it more than all temporal evils, because the smallest injury done to him is infinitely greater than the most serious misfortune that can befall his creatures.

Nothing can justify the commission of a venial sin. If any circumstance could make it lawful, it would not be a sin. Were the conversion or salvation of the whole world at stake, God would be offended at the most trivial lie told to effect it. If, by committing a venial sin, I could procure the greatest possible glory to God, he would accept it on no such condition.

It is an article of faith, that I can never enter heaven so long as my soul is infected with the least venial stain, *for nothing defiled can enter heaven.* (Apoc. xxi.) Whatever may be the merit of my life in other respects, if my soul, at its departure from my body, be defiled with only one venial sin uneffaced by repentance, my happiness will be retarded, and my soul will not be admitted into the bosom of the Deity until it has passed through the purifying flames of purgatory.

The severity with which the Almighty has often punished venial sin in this life clearly proves the hatred that he bears to it. We know by the testimony of Holy Scripture that, in punishment of a sin of vanity in king David, the entire race of the chosen people of God was nearly annihilated; and that a Levite, who presumed merely to touch the ark of the covenant, was instantly struck dead.* Oh! it is a strange infatuation in me, to commit venial sin with so little remorse, and to make so light of the punishment which awaits it. But it is a thousand times more deplorable, that I make no more grateful return to God for all his goodness to

---

* Although Father Bourdaloue supposes the two sins here mentioned to be only *venial*, the reader is, of course, free to entertain another opinion.

me, than to give him the most trivial wilful offence.

SECOND POINT.—How numerous are my venial sins! May I not say with David, that *they are multiplied beyond the number of the hairs of my head?* (Ps. xxxix.) I see not all the faults which occur in my slothful and imperfect life; but it ought to be a source of inconsolable grief to me, to know that God clearly sees them all, and that, were he to expose them to my view, I should find them to be innumerable.

How frequently do I commit venial sins by forgetfulness of my duty—by neglecting to study it—by my indocility in receiving friendly admonitions—and by presumptuously trusting to my own lights? How often do I sin by imprudence or inadvertence arising from dissipation of mind—from levity of disposition—from the unguarded use of my tongue—and from rash judgments and groundless suspicions? How often do I commit sins of frailty by habitual self-indulgence—by neglect of method and order in my various occupations—by following the suggestions of nature, and refusing to do violence to my temper or inclinations? How many imperfections may I not by a little attention discover in the celebration of the holy mysteries—in the recital of my office—in the performance of the duties of the confessional—

in the preparation of my sermons and instructions—in my endeavours to reclaim sinners—and in every other part of my duty?

How often do I, even on very trivial occasions, commit venial sins with full deliberation and malice, perhaps stifling the remorse of my conscience by the reflection, that venial sin does not merit eternal punishment? All this proves my indifference towards God, and my insensibility to every thing but my own interest. Did I truly love God, a knowledge of the moral impossibility of avoiding all venial sin, and of the fatal necessity, under which all men labour, of offending in many things, would cause me frequently to exclaim with St. Paul in the anguish of sincere grief: *wretch that I am, who will deliver me from the body of this death!* (Rom. vii.) But, after all, it is certain, that there is no particular venial sin which it is not in my power to avoid. How greatly, then, might the number of my sins be diminished by my using proper precaution?

THIRD POINT.—My dread of venial sin will be increased by the consideration of its terrible consequences. As corporal sickness is the forerunner of death, so is venial sin the high road to mortal. A true value, consequently, for my soul will induce me to use the same degree of caution against venial sin that I should against an attack of sickness.

Knowing that a bodily infirmity, if neglected, may terminate in death, I hesitate not to apply prompt, efficacious, and, if necessary, even violent remedies, with the view of saving my life. Why, then, do I not adopt the same reasonable principle with reference to those spiritual disorders, which, if disregarded, will certainly lead to that second and eternal death, a thousand times more terrible than the death of the body?

It is a truth founded on the infallible testimony of the Word of God and confirmed by constant experience, that the disregard, and much more the contempt, of venial sin, is the certain road to mortal. Familiarity with the one diminishes and soon destroys the horror which a soul in grace entertains of the other. Besides, the line of separation between mortal and venial sin is oftentimes so indistinct as to be almost imperceptible; the most learned divines are not unfrequently at a loss to define it; in many cases, a little more or less decides the whole difference between life and death eternal. Oh! how dangerous it is to walk on the border of a precipice!

In consequence of the proximity existing between mortal and venial sin, nothing is more natural than that the one should often be mistaken for the other. Have I never deceived myself by regarding as trivial what in reality was not so? Have I, on no occasion, framed to myself a false conscience, by

THIRD MEDITATION. 25

judging of things rather according by the desires of my own heart, than by the maxims of the divine law? The difficulty of discriminating between mortal and venial sin renders it highly necessary ever to preserve a timorous conscience.

But, supposing myself endowed with sufficient light to distinguish on all occasions where venial terminates and mortal sin begins, is it not the greatest presumption in me, who am the very essence of weakness, to think myself so strongly fortified against the influence of corrupt nature, and so far master of my own heart, as to be able to prescribe to it such bounds as I please? Under many temptations a particular grace is necessary to keep me from falling; and I ought to be aware, that a frequent and just punishment of a disregard of venial sin is the refusal, on the part of God, of this special grace in the hour of need. It is thus that venial sin may be, and to thousands of souls really is, the cause of damnation.

CONCLUDING PRAYER. — Enable me, O God, to love and observe thy law in its greatest perfection. I know that, the farther I advance in virtue, in the less danger I am of falling, and that, the more I aspire to fidelity in little things, the less I shall be disposed to transgress in essential duties. Still, notwithstanding the resolutions which I now make through thy grace, and in thy presence, I dare not promise always to keep myself perfectly innocent. So long as I remain invested with this mortal body, I fear that I shall too often experience the sorrowful effects of human frailty. But I know that the best security against mortal sin is, to strive, on all occasions, rather to exceed than to fall short of what is of strict obligation, and to try daily to advance in perfection. This, therefore, is what I sincerely propose to do.

Grant me, O God, a timorous conscience, one that will always take the alarm at the very shadow of sin, without stopping to inquire whether it be mortal or venial. I am aware that I must, on many occasions, deny to nature what it craves, and refuse myself many apparently innocent gratifications; I see that, under any circumstances, I must restrain the emotions of my heart, put a door of circumspection upon my lips, captivate my eyes, and mortify my senses; but, my God, I am withal sensible, that I cannot purchase at too dear a rate the double advantage of offending thee less, and of placing my salvation in greater security. The happiness of pleasing thee, and the peace of a good conscience will abundantly compensate for every sacrifice that I shall be required to make.

CONSIDERATION.

ON THE PERFECTION OF OUR ORDINARY ACTIONS.

FIRST POINT.—I am not to suppose that perfection consists in doing a multiplicity of things. This idea was the error of Martha, so pointedly condemned by Jesus Christ. Neither does it require the performance of things great and extraordinary. Many have been great saints in the sight of God, who have done nothing extraordinary for him, and whose actions were devoid of all external show and splendour. Their sanctity was great, though employed about things which the worlds esteems little. By their fidelity in the performance of these trivial things they acquired infinite treasures of merit. They were great principally by their humility, which prompted them to leave to others such employments as are calculated to attract notice and esteem, and to choose for themselves occupations mean and contemptible. In short, from the very circumstance of extraordinary actions being necessarily of rare occurrence, I may be certain that perfection cannot consist in them. It must consist in something habitual, something which I have continually in hand, and which fills up the days and years of my life.

Hence I am to infer, that perfection consists in the faithful performance of the duties of the state of life, to which God has called me. It is certain, that in the accomplishment of the will of God consists the essence of sanctity—that this motive gives a value and dignity to all that I do—that without it my most splendid performances are nothing—and that with it the meanest are of transcendent merit. I may, therefore, lay it down as a most undoubted truth, that I never can be perfect in the sight of God, but by the faithful discharge of my ordinary duties. For thirty years of his life Jesus Christ did nothing that could gain him the esteem of men; all his actions appeared mean and trivial to human eyes; but, because *he did in all things the will of his Father* (John viii.), his performances were objects of infinite complacency in his sight.

What a source of consolation are these truths to me! I need not go far to seek perfection: it is at hand; it is within me; I shall find it in my daily occupations. Although my situation may be greatly inferior to the talents which I possess, yet, in doing the will of my superiors in the most humble situation, I have more merit in the sight of God than I should have in a place of my own selection, and which I might suppose better suited to my abilities. To aim at perfection in this way is a thing pleasing both to God and men; for men even are edified by it, and by that means virtue is brought into credit and esteem.—It may be thought easy thus to walk in the path of humble obedience. In speculation it is so; but long perseverance in this way, with uniform fidelity and constancy, is a work of some difficulty, and requires violence to be done to human nature.

SECOND POINT.—The mere discharge of my duty will not make me perfect. I must do it well, that is, with exactness, fervour, and perseverance, so that what was said of Jesus Christ may be applicable to me: *he hath done all things well.* (Mark vii.)—1st, with *exactness*, by not willfully omitting the least part of what is required of me. This exactness comprises the time, the place, and the manner of action, a want of fidelity in any one of which would be a transgression of the divine will, and would diminish the value and merit of my performance.—2nd, with *fervour:* this does not mean that a sensible relish and pleasure must necessarily accompany the discharge of my duty, for these, although the ordinary accompaniments of fervour, are by no means inseparable from it. I may be very fervent, and yet feel a natural disgust, dryness, and repugnance in the performance of my duty. Fervour, indeed, is far more solid and meritorious when it impels me to act with resolution in spite of natural coldness and antipathy.—3rd, with *perseverance:* of all requisites this is the most difficult of attainment. What St. Bernard said of a religious life compared with martyrdom, is still more applicable to my vocation, viz.: that, "to regard any one particular exercise of a religious life, there is no proportion between it and martyrdom; yet, to consider the assemblage of them all, and their duration to the end of life, they are much more repugnant and insupportable to nature." "Hence," he continues, "it is not unusual to see monks, and even Christians, in the world" (and, I may add, pastors of souls also) "exact in fulfilling their duties for a time or on certain days; but it is a thing of rare occurrence to find one, who ever walks on with an even pace, without hesitation or change— who labours to-day with the same assiduity as yesterday—and who never relaxes in the fervent discharge of his duties to the last moment of his life. Constancy like this, wherever found, will, indeed, bear a comparison with the fortitude of the martyrs under their torments." The lesson contained in this remark of St. Bernard is worthy of my serious consideration. When I reflect on the import of these three rules, have I not occasion to be confounded and to tremble at the little progress that I have made in perfection?

THIRD POINT.—The last degree of perfection required to be given to my actions, and which is, as it were, the soul and life of them, is to perform them with a true internal spirit, and through a motive of religion. Any thing without this is but the external part of sanctity. What gives life to my works, and consecrates them to God, is the motive and intention with which they are done. To acquit myself of my daily actions through humour, fancy, inclination, custom, human respect, ostentation, or interest, is not doing them for God; and upon no such terms will he receive them or place them to account. Were I, therefore, to perform the most heroic acts of virtue, and not refer them to him, he would regard them, to say the least, with indifference; not being directed to his glory, they would produce no fruit for me.

These are serious truths for my meditation. For, if I take a review of the actions of my past life, and examine them by this rule, how many shall I find whereon to ground a favourable calculation? It is true, I comply with the external part of my duty; I perform my private and public devotions; I am not remiss in instructing the ignorant, in administering the sacraments, in endeavouring to reclaim sinners, and in visiting the sick; but do I not go through these sacred duties without referring them to God—through mere custom—often with a levity of mind and dissipation of heart that cannot but stifle every pious sentiment—perhaps, sometimes, even purely to save appearances, or through a desire of being noticed and esteemed? And what is all this in the sight of God? With reference to my progress in perfection, it is no more than if I had left the whole undone.

My misfortune is the greater and my neglect the more to be condemned, because there was nothing in all my performances, which might not have been referred to God; for, it is not so much my actions themselves that he regards, as the spirit with which they are done. How admirable is here his wisdom and how amiable his providence! He has not given equal talents to all; he has not called all to occupations equally important; but, because he has called all to perfection he has decreed that not a single action, however mean and obscure, shall be excluded from merit proportioned to the uprightness and purity of intention with which it is performed. With such facilities for growing rich in virtue and merit, how lamentable is it that I should be so poor and destitute!— Every action of my life might have been profitable to me, and I am not sure that a single one has found acceptance with God, and been of benefit to my soul. What can I do but regret and repent of the past, and redouble my care and diligence for the future?

Second Day.

FIRST MEDITATION.

ON SCANDAL AND GOOD EXAMPLE.

It is necessary that scandal should come.—MAT. xviii.

FIRST POINT.—It can neither be denied nor concealed, that in every state, not excepting that of the priesthood, instances of scandal or bad example sometimes occur. If a traitor was found amongst the apostles selected by Jesus Christ, it cannot appear surprising that, amongst their numerous successors in the holy ministry, there should occasionally exist traitors to the sacred cause in which they are engaged. Considering the diversity of dispositions, sentiments, and manners amongst men, it is morally impossible that some should not be found, whose laxity and disorders become an occasion of temptation and fall to others. But, when there are any such amongst the ministers of the altar, it is an evil great beyond all comparison in itself, and most terrible in its consequences.

Great, indeed, must be the crime of scandal from the divine anathemas pronounced against it. *Woe to him by whom scandal cometh.* (Mat. xviii.) This malediction proceeds from the lips of Jesus Christ, who adds: *it were better for a man, that a mill-stone were tied round his neck and he were cast into the depth of the sea,* than that he should be guilty of it. No person is excepted from this general and universal maxim; but it applies especially to pastors of souls, who above all others are commanded, *so to let their light shine before men, that others, seeing their good works, may glorify their Father who is in heaven* (Mat. v.). Woe, then, to me, if I deprive my state of one of its most precious advantages, by becoming an occasion of sin to those whom my vocation particularly obliges me to edify. Woe to me, if I lead astray even one of those, who, from the authority, credit, and talents which I have received from God, look up to me as their guide. If my life be irregular, what shall I be able to answer, when the Almighty shall point out to me the injury which religion has thereby sustained?

The absence of every thing glaringly immoral in my life and actions is not a decisive proof, that I am free from the guilt of scandal. If I do not possess that degree of perfection in every Christian virtue, which the Almighty designs that I should preach both by word and example, and which the faithful, in fact, expect to find in me, I become a subject of scandal to them. Thus, if I ever make use of language bordering upon the profane—if I evince a spirit of avarice by too rigorous an exaction of what I consider my due—if I indulge in too familiar conversation with persons of the other sex—if I shew by my conduct, or express in words, enmity against another—if I am proud and vain-glorious in my actions or discourse—if I am a lover of good cheer, and make it the frequent topic of conversation—if I am addicted to anger, passion, or impatience—if I restrain not even my innocent recreations within due bounds, and shew a passion for the vain amusements and pastimes of the world—if I celebrate the holy sacrifice hastily and without external marks of reverence and piety—if I am slothful in performing any part of my duty—if I allude indiscreetly to matters connected with the sacred tribunal—if I violate the laws of fraternal charity by back-biting or detraction—nay, if I do any thing not unlawful in itself, yet not commanded, but which I know that others, through ignorance, will regard as sinful—I may, on any of these occasions, give grievous scandal.

Have I hitherto been sufficiently cautious and circumspect in all these points? Have I been careful never to say or do any thing, which in its nature was calculated to prejudice those who heard me, or were witnesses of my actions? Have I never advanced maxims, given advice, or otherwise inspired sentiments or approved of proceedings, opposed to the true spirit of religion or morality? If so, I have been guilty of scandal; and, have I thought of declaring that circumstance in confession, and repairing the scandal given? Perhaps, oftentimes I have neither thought of the one nor the other. But was my inadvertency excusable? Was it not the natural consequence of an indolent and careless life? Be this as it may, I have occasion to pray with the prophet: *From my hidden sins cleanse me, O Lord, and for the sins of others spare thy servant* (Ps. xvii.).

SECOND POINT.—Scandal may not only be given, but likewise taken ; and, as to give scandal is a crime, so it will be no excuse for any defects in my life, to say that I followed the example of others. The example of Lucifer drew other angels into apostasy, but they were condemned along with him. My only lawful model is Jesus Christ, and his Gospel is my only rule. It will, therefore, avail me nothing to allege that, instead of copying him and adhering to his Gospel, I took the example of others for my guide.

Bad example is a temptation, and oftentimes a very strong one; yet, as long as I have the means of overcoming it, to yield to it must always be a sin. The rules which I should follow, in order to avoid falling into the snares of scandal, are, 1st, not to be too much dejected at witnessing the faults or imperfections of one or other of my brethren : for, since Jesus Christ has foretold that such scandals must exist, I need not be surprised when I see them happen :—2nd, I must try to turn the scandal to my own spiritual profit, by taking occasion therefrom to renew my protestations of inviolable fidelity and attachment to the holy laws of God :—3rd, I must avoid, as much as possible, the society of those whose principles or conduct are disedifying, and by no means make them my associates and confidants:—4th, I must oppose and condemn what is wrong, prudently, but resolutely—with charity, but regardless of human respect :—lastly, I must endeavour to draw from the scandal itself an occasion of humbling myself before God, acknowledging that of myself I am all weakness and imperfection, and that, but for the incessant supplies of his grace, I should be even worse than others.

THIRD POINT.—As the pastor who gives scandal is accursed, so, blessed is the priest who sets good example, and blessed is the flock to which the Almighty gives a pastor according to his own heart. Under him the crooked paths are made straight, and the

FIRST MEDITATION.

rough ways plain, and all flesh sees the salvation of God. By him the kingdom of Jesus Christ is established on the ruins of the empire of Satan, and those, who were sitting in darkness and the shades of death, are led into the way of truth and life. Happy, then, am I, if, like my heavenly Master, I serve as a living Gospel to the ignorant, and my life as well as my tongue speak reproof to the slothful and the wicked. When I walk without blame in the ways of the Lord—when I am assiduous in prayer, and zealously devoted to the duties of my ministry—when I exhibit in my life a contempt for all earthly things, and a love of humility and the cross—when I make myself all to all and shew that I am ready upon occasion even to lay down my life for my sheep—then will they listen to my voice and cheerfully obey my call; then will they learn truly to hate vice, and will become enamoured of virtue, rendered charming in their eyes by my example. Thus will my light shine, as it ought to do, before men, who, seeing my good works, will, by their own lives, give glory to my heavenly Father.

CONCLUDING PRAYER.—Grant, O my God, that it may never be my misfortune to lead those astray, by evil example, whom thou hast commissioned me to guide to thee. Let nothing in my life henceforth contradict those sacred and sublime maxims of morality, of which I am an appointed teacher. I cannot but tremble when I reflect on the many occasions of my past life, on which it is much to be feared, that my example has diverted others from thy service, and my sloth has occasioned the fervour of many to grow cool. Ah! my God, did I embrace the priesthood only thereby to bring damnation upon the souls of others, and a tenfold damnation upon my own? But, whatever may have been my past misfortune, I know that it is not irreparable, and, therefore, I am determined to take effectual measures during this Retreat to repair it. *I have said, now I begin:* oh that this may be the *change* of thy *right hand*.

Strengthen, also, I beseech thee, my weakness, that I may never be led astray by the laxity of others. Enlighten my mind to a clear understanding of thy holy law, and let me, on all occasions, remember, that neither the example nor the counsel of others, but thy pure Gospel, is my rule. Make me fly the company of such as would withdraw me from following it, and give me discretion to select those only for my familiar friends, who will spur me on by word and example to embrace it.

SECOND MEDITATION.

ON SPIRITUAL SLOTH.

Because thou art neither hot nor cold, I will begin to vomit thee out of my mouth.—APOC. iii.

FIRST POINT.—In my state are to be found persons, who have the name only, and not the spirit, of their profession ; who, after taking upon their shoulders the yoke of Jesus Christ, try to throw it off ; who live without compunction ; whose thoughts are carnal and worldly ; who pray without devotion, and read without edification. These persons are slothful. It concerns me much to examine, whether I be of their number.

Great is the danger of spiritual sloth, because those who are involved in it are not aware of their state, and consequently live on without remorse. This insensibility proceeds from two causes :—1st, instead of examining their consciences on the sins which they commit, and the good which they leave undone, they attend only to the sins which they do not commit, and what little good they happen to do,—and, 2nd, instead of comparing their lives with the lives of the truly fervent and devout, they calm the reproaches of conscience by reflecting, that there are others worse than themselves. Thus it often comes to pass, that, slothful as they are, the testimony of their consciences is as favourable as though they really fulfilled all justice.

So terrible is the state of sloth, that, according to the assurance of the Spirit of God, a worse or more guilty one would be preferable to it. Truly it would be better for many souls to fall into mortal sin, than into tepidity. Mortal sin would be followed by remorse of conscience; and, in a favourable moment, the ordinary grace of God would effect their conversion. But the tepid and slothful have no remorse of conscience—they have no scruple about their state. Hence, all who are experienced in spiritual things agree, that it is more difficult to arise from sloth, than from vice and licentiousness. Cassian, amongst others, testifies, that he had known many worldlings, after their conversion, become fervent and spiritual, but that he had never witnessed a similar change in a religious man, who had fallen into a habit of sloth. How ought this testimony to make me tremble?

Another misfortune attending sloth is, that it renders the yoke of the Lord, which of itself is light and sweet, heavy and insupportable. Whilst the fervent soul has its burthen lightened by the sweet unction of divine grace, the tepid groans under its entire weight. Thus does God, even in this life, suffer the crime of sloth to be its own punishment. But divine justice does not stop here : for the Almighty, in his horror of the slothful soul, declares that he *begins to vomit it out of his mouth.* This he does by withdrawing himself gradually farther and farther from it. Sloth, therefore, may justly be termed the commencement of final reprobation. What more than this can be required to rouse me from it ? Shall I delay until God has entirely abandoned me ?

SECOND POINT.—The true causes of sloth are to be found within myself ; for I cannot become slothful except by the free consent of my own will. To attribute it to God would be the height of injustice. God not unfrequently permits souls to fall into a state of dryness, in order to purify them, to disengage their affections from sensible things, and to perfect them in his love. But dryness and tepidity are not to be confounded together. The soul in a state of aridity knows and bewails its misfortune ; but the slothful soul is insensible to its misery.

One of the causes, then, of sloth, is the careless omission of the ordinary exercises of piety, such as prayer, spiritual reading, the use of the sacraments, the daily examination of conscience, and works of mortification and penance. When a trifling impediment is admitted as a pretext for deferring these exercises to a more convenient time, that time seldom arrives. Occasional omissions soon lead to habitual neglect. Does not my conscience here plead guilty? Have I not many times put God by for the world, and, under some frivolous pretext or other, abandoned my spiritual exercises? If so, I cannot be surprised at having fallen into a state of tepidity. I must lose the spirit of fervour and piety, if I take no pains to preserve it.

The first steps to sloth, however, are not generally the entire neglect of any part of our religious exercises, but the careless performance of them. A habit of mental dissipation thereby gradually acquired, soon destroys the spirit of internal recollection; for it is impossible that a person, who suffers his mind to be continually engaged by exterior objects, should not by degrees lose his zeal for perfection; and sloth ever gains ground in the same proportion that zeal and fervour die away. Am I not convinced, by my own experience, that this is true?

But, after all, sloth in its greatest, although most remote cause, is to be attributed to a disregard for small things. Instead of being feelingly sensible that nothing is trivial that relates to God and his worship,—that perfection consists not so much in great things as in the manner of doing those which are less,—that fidelity in lesser things is a source of great merit,—and that, to maintain fidelity in what is great, it is necessary to be faithful in that which is small;—instead of being guided by these principles, a person is apt to grow weary with observances apparently of little moment; and thus neglecting them one after another, he, at length, becomes involved in confirmed tepidity. If, from the time I was first made acquainted with these truths, I had always been guided by them, I might now be far advanced in virtue; whereas, it is well if I am not farther removed from perfection than when I began to serve God.

Third Point.—Difficult as it is to cure spiritual sloth, with the grace of God it is not absolutely irremediable; and though the instances of cure be few, it is the will of the Almighty that I should be one. With this view he has inspired me with the desire of making the present Retreat. The remedies of tepidity may be divided into two kinds, the first consisting in pure reflection, the second in practice.

1st, I must reflect frequently and seriously on the greatness and dignity of the God in whose service I am engaged; on what he is to me, and what I am to him. He is my sovereign Lord, my judge, and my creator. I am his subject, his slave, his creature.— This motive St. Paul employed to excite fervour in the primitive Christians: *I conjure you to walk in the way of God, in a manner worthy of God* (Coll. i.). To endeavour to think, to speak, to pray, to labour, and to live at all times *in a manner worthy of God*, will assuredly be found an infallible remedy for sloth. 2d, The deportment of worldlings towards persons of rank ought to be a continual lesson to me, and should make me blush to think that, whilst they do so much to honour the great ones of the earth, I have so little zeal for the honour and glory of the eternal King of earth and heaven. 3d, I should reflect on the inestimable benefit that I shall derive from every action performed with fervour; that whatever I do is capable of meriting an eternal recompense; and that this recompense will be proportioned to my dispositions. By these and similar considerations, the saints kept alive in their breasts the fire of fervent piety.

The practical remedy for sloth is to destroy the cause by cultivating the virtues opposed to it. Thus, I must immediately resume with great exactness and assiduity the exercises which sloth has occasioned me to omit. I must be determined, and use the utmost diligence, not to fail in the most trifling point of duty, to surmount all difficulties, and to overcome whatever natural repugnance I may feel; being willing, if it so please God, to serve him all my life without unction or consolation, and esteeming it but too great a happiness to be admitted again into his service on any terms.

CONCLUDING PRAYER.—In this disposition of heart, I come to thee, O God, with humble confidence, that, notwithstanding my past sloth, thou hast not entirely cast me off. From the strong call with which thou hast this day favoured me, I cannot doubt of thy desire to reconduct me into the paths of fidelity and obedience, and to restore me once more to the state of fervour from which I have fallen. Give me grace to accomplish thy will and to execute my purposes.

It is not, O Lord, the first time that I have made similar resolutions ; and will my present purposes be more effectual than former ones ? I know that, from my own weakness and inconstancy of mind I have much to fear; but I have everything to hope from thy mercy and goodness. O my God, is it not time that I should begin to serve thee as I ought ? Am I always to remain buried in sloth ? Are all my days to be passed in imperfection and irregularity, without fruit or merit ? Enable me to profit by the admonition which thou hast this day given me, and by the reproaches of my own conscience. May I now begin, once for all, in good earnest, lest, by further delay, my tepidity should terminate in confirmed blindness and obduracy of heart. Forbid, O God, that so awful a judgment should ever befall me. By thy grace, I this day enter upon a new life; and, by the same, I will persevere in it to the end.

THIRD MEDITATION.

ON THE ABUSE OF GRACE.

We exhort you, not to receive the grace of God in vain.—1 COR. vi.

FIRST POINT.—The supernatural helps, which I receive from Almighty God, are talents lent in order to be improved; and faith teaches that he will demand an account of each of them, because each grace ought to produce fruit, and to enhance the glory of the giver: *Lord, thou hast given me five talents*, said the good servant to his master; *behold, I have gained other five* (Matt. xxx.).

From this it follows that the more graces God favours me with the more humble and fervent I ought to be—humble, because these graces are not my own, and I am accountable for them:—and fervent, because it is only thus I can discharge the immense debt which I owe to God for his infinite goodness.

THIRD MEDITATION. 49

It is certain that, as a priest, I have received more abundant and special graces than the common faithful. The consequence of this is, that I have much more to account for than other Christians, and that from me much more is expected than from them.

Oftentimes, perhaps, have I admonished the rich, of the great occasion they have to tremble at the responsibility attached to the possession of wealth; but I have much more reason to tremble for myself in contemplating the invaluable treasures of spiritual wealth confided to me. Why did Jesus Christ weep over Jerusalem? Not because of the temporal punishment, which his Father was preparing for that unhappy city: his compassion was moved by the foresight of the dreadful spiritual calamities and woes, with which the abuse of so many special graces was shortly to be followed, in the total rejection of this his once chosen people. Have I not reason to apprehend a similar judgment, as the just punishment of my repeated infidelities to divine grace?

The reprobate in hell will eternally lament their abuse of grace; they will eternally wish it were in their power to repair their loss; but it will be the completion of their despair to know that their loss is irreparable. In that abode of eternal woe are thousands of my predecessors in the sacred ministry, who are paying the penalty justly due to the abuse of divine grace. This misfortune should be a warning to me. Oh! how thankful ought I to be to the Almighty, that I have yet a resource against his rigorous justice in a life of penance and the proper use of present graces!

SECOND POINT.—Of graces some are exterior, others interior. Exterior graces are the means furnished by God in order to my salvation. In every period of my life he has lavished these graces upon me; and what use have I made of them? After having spent several years in an asylum of virtue and religion, what better am I than hundreds of Christians, who have never enjoyed this advantage, but have always been surrounded by, and obliged to contend with, the dangers and temptations of the world? Where is the fruit of all the meditations, confessions, and communions, which I made during the time of my preparation for the holy ministry? What benefit have I derived from the instructions, exhortations, and good example, that I then received? If I have abused all these graces, I never can sufficiently bewail my misfortune; and if I repent not, the judgment of an angry God will be proportioned to the extraordinary means of salvation which he has provided for me. *Let the barren fig-tree be cut down* (said the Master in the Gospel); *why cumbereth it the ground?* (Luke xiii.). Perhaps I am this barren fig-tree; and, if so, I see what I have to expect from continuing to abuse the grace of God.

The means of salvation, which I enjoy, have sanctified thousands in my state of life, but they have neither made me more exact, more vigilant, more dead to the world and myself, nor in respect more perfect, than if I had not received them. These means were sufficient to have converted entire nations of idolaters; but in me they have neither corrected a single fault nor produced a single virtue. *Woe to thee, Corozain, woe to thee, Bethsaida; for if in Tyre and Sidon had been wrought the things that have been wrought in thee, they had long since done penance in sack-cloth and ashes* (Mat. xi.). If I have abused the divine grace, this terrible malediction is applicable to me. I shall be made accountable not merely for the non-application of these salutary means, but for having perverted them into occasions of sin. By receiving them in vain I add to my measure of guilt. Oh! what treasure of wrath have I been storing up to myself against the day of wrath! And instead of trying to diminish, am I not still daily augmenting, the store?

THIRD POINT.—Interior graces are those inward operations of the Holy Ghost, whereby he makes known to me his ways, and inclines me to love them—the lights which he communicates to my soul—the good desires with which he inspires me—the remorse of conscience with which he visits me—and the solicitations whereby he presses me to change my conduct, to be more exact in all my duties, and to lead a more religious life. I cannot say that I have not been favoured with such graces; and, by resisting them, I have resisted the Holy Spirit, trodden under foot the blood of Jesus Christ, and annihilated, in my regard, the merits of his cross.

Should I continue any longer unfaithful to these graces, I have no other to expect than the subtraction of them; for nothing can be more just than that what I disregard should be taken away, what I despise should be withdrawn. Ah! this would indeed be judgment without mercy—a pure evil, without any alloy of good. Perhaps I have already, in some degree, incurred this dreadful curse; and I may conclude that such is really the case, if I perceive myself less sensible than heretofore to the reproaches of conscience, and live on in tranquillity and peace, whilst I cannot but know that my life is full of imperfection and sloth.

God sometimes grants to us special and extraordinary calls, which, in the order of salvation, may be compared to that critical moment in the order of nature, which decides a person's recovery from, or his falling a victim to, a corporal malady. Such are certain particular days and times of salvation provided for us by his gracious Providence; and probably these very days of solitude and retreat are such for me. The abuse of this grace, then, would be to put the last seal to my reprobation. St. Augustine and thousands of other penitents would have been eternally lost, had they suffered the hour of their particular visitation to pass by. In like manner, many have fallen into the most lamentable disorders, in consequence of not having availed themselves of certain favourable circumstances, in which the Almighty solicited them to resume the care of their salvation.

CONCLUDING PRAYER. — Blessed, O Lord, by thy infinite goodness, that, notwithstanding my repeated abuse of thy gracious calls, thou hast not yet abandoned me. I now hear thy voice speaking to my interior, and I am determined to be no longer rebellious to it, and thus to run on with obstinate blindness to my eternal ruin.

Praised a thousand times, O my God, be thy gracious Providence for the means ordained by it for my sanctification. Never can I sufficiently testify my sincere and affectionate gratitude for all thy mercies to me. My continual abuse of thy grace is to me a source of the most heartfelt grief, and oh! may thy infinite goodness forbid that it should be for me hereafter a never-ending subject of confusion and fruitless repentance.

Hitherto, O Lord, in contemplating the causes of thy severe but just judgments, I have regarded nothing but my positive transgressions of thy law; but now I am sensible that I have much more to fear from the abuse of thy grace, without which my transgressions would not be imputed to me, and I should have a secure shelter against thy vengeance. Ought I, then, to pray to thee to interrupt henceforth the streams of thy grace? O Lord! what could I do without thee? No, my God, do not interrupt those streams, but rather let them flow still more abundantly, for they are the only foundation of my hope. As far as depends on me, I am determined, from this time forward, never to place any obstacle to the current of thy grace, to prescribe no limits to my correspondence with the good designs with which thou mayest be pleased to inspire me, and to serve thee, on all occasions, according to the full extent and efficacy of the helps with which thy mercy and goodness may supply me. These, O God, are my purposes, and in further confirmation of them I will venture to adopt the language of thy holy and fervent prophet: *I swear and resolve to keep thy laws* (Ps. cxviii.).

CONSIDERATION.

ON MENTAL PRAYER.

The reflections on mental prayer may be reduced to three points : 1st, Its advantages ; 2d, The defects which prevent its producing fruit ; and 3d, The pretexts usually alleged for the omission of it.

FIRST POINT.—The advantages and importance of mental prayer.—It is essential to my sanctification that my mind be impressed with a lively apprehension of the maxims of the gospel, and of the great truths of Christianity ; for, *the just man lives by faith* (Rom. i.). So universally is this principle acknowledged, that even worldlings confess that their lives would be free from numberless errors to which they are subject, were their faith more lively and their minds more thoroughly penetrated with the gospel truths. Self-examination will convince me that this want of a lively faith is the cause of my laxity, as it is, also, of those of my state in general.

This evil can be remedied only by the use of mental prayer. By tracing in my mind the truths of religion—by meditating on the greatness and perfections of the Deity, his mercy and his justice, his rewards and his punishments—by considering in order and succession all the mysteries of Jesus Christ, his doctrine, his law, his morality, and his example, and trying to deduce from them lessons for my own conduct, just and exalted ideas of religion will become deeply engraven on my soul. These will remind me, in the various occurrences of life, of what I owe to God, to my neighbour and to myself: new lights will burst in upon me, and I shall discover errors, illusions, and false opinions, of which I was previously ignorant. Grace will then come in to my support and diffuse its light in an abundance proportioned to the frequency and fervour of my prayer; so that many truths, at first but imperfectly understood, will daily become more fully developed, and, at length, represented before me with a clearness amounting almost to demonstration.

From the intimate connexion between the mind and the heart, the latter necessarily becomes inflamed by meditation. The soul then elevates itself to God—it grows enamoured of its duty—it reproaches itself with its past infidelities—it takes the requisite measures for amendment—and, ultimately, it finds itself quite changed and renewed. By this means the saints attained perfection; and, if I **really** aspire to an imitation of their sanctity, I must walk in the path marked out by them. They were all assiduous in mental prayer. However much the great masters of an interior life have varied in their prescriptions of religious exercises, on the absolute necessity of meditation they are universally agreed. In fact, they lay it down as the very soul of a Christian life, and regard the constant and persevering practice of it as one of the most unequivocal marks of divine grace, and the habitual neglect of it as an undoubted sign of reprobation.

It is next to impossible that a soul assiduous in mental prayer should go astray; or if, in an unguarded moment, it should happen to be surprised and fall into sin, it finds an infallible resource in prayer. I was instructed, at an early age, in the utility and necessity of this holy exercise, and was brought up in the practice of it: and if, since my entrance into the world, my fervour has cooled, and I have receded instead of having advanced in virtue, to what other cause can this misfortune be attributed, but to the neglect and omission of mental prayer? Through this, many in my state of life fall into dryness, sloth, and insensibility to the things of God, so that their hearts never feel the moving truths of religion, which they are continually inculcating to others; and what wonder if, being deprived of the consolations of religion, of the copious supplies of divine grace, and of all, in short, that is requisite to support them under their difficulties, trials, and temptations, they grow disgusted with their duties, and, in the end, became easy victims of the devil and their passions?

SECOND POINT.—The ordinary defects in mental prayer are, first, the disregard of that injunction of the Holy Spirit: *before prayer prepare thy soul, and be not like a man that tempteth God.* — (Eccle. xviii.) To expect divine communications without disposing ourselves to receive them, is equivalent to asking the Almighty to alter the ordinary conduct of his Providence, and to perform a miracle in our favour. The preparation for prayer is two-fold: there is a distant and an immediate preparation. The former consists in habitual recollection, and in cultivating, as far as is consistent with our state of life, a spirit of retirement: the latter, in the previous selection and arrangement of the subject for meditation, placing ourselves in the presence of God, invoking the light of his Holy Spirit, and removing ourselves from every direct source of distraction.

Secondly, many undertake their meditation without a serious wish to profit by it; and, provided a few transient sentiments of devotion enter their minds during a certain time apportioned to this exercise, they are quite content. But *wisdom*—that heavenly wisdom, which enlightens and sanctifies the soul—*communicates herself only to those who desire and seek for her* (Eccl. iv.).

Thirdly, Some begin their prayer without any particular subject, leaving their minds and hearts, as they pretend, to the impulse of the Spirit of God. To grant, however, such impulse is not an ordinary operation of that divine Spirit, but an extraordinary grace, on which no one is authorized to calculate, as, indeed, it is seldom granted, except to humble souls long exercised in the ordinary way.

Fourthly, Others, not reflecting that the best prayer is that which advances a person most in the virtues of humility, charity, patience, and mortification, do not attempt to go beyond a few speculative reflections, which tend to no practical effect.

Fifthly, After the selection of a proper subject, it is a common omission to be satisfied with mere reasoning and reflection, without proceeding to affections and resolutions. It will, however, be of little avail towards the great end of meditation to have the mind convinced, unless the heart be likewise moved. The heart is the seat of good resolutions, and these are the forerunners of action.

Sixthly, With reference to our resolutions themselves, it is a common but dangerous error, to make them only in general terms; whereas, it is of the last importance that a person descend to particulars, and direct his resolution to those points which, under present circumstances, demand his attention.

Lastly, The capital defect of mental prayer, and which is the principal obstacle to its producing fruit, is to live in a state of habitual sloth and negligence, without endeavouring to surmount it. Prayer requires application, and this costs more trouble than the slothful are willing to bestow; for nature does not like to do violence to itself. But it is folly to expect that God will bless the prayer of him who remains careless and indifferent.

Third Point.—Various excuses are alleged for the omission of mental prayer. Some say they have not time for it—others that they cannot perform it without distraction—others, again, that they experience nothing but dryness in the exercise of it—many pretend that it tires and disgusts them—and, in short, many think it above their capacity.

As to the first, so far from the multiplicity of a person's affairs being a lawful plea for the omission of mental prayer, it in reality imposes upon him the stricter obligation of entering frequently into himself, and using prayer as a preventive of that dissipation of mind, which external occupations (no matter of what kind they may be) will otherwise necessarily produce. The more the saints were burthened with cares, and those even of a spiritual kind, the greater need they felt of prayer. The urgency of duty, or even the claims of civility, in the life of a Pastor, may occasionally render the omission of prayer expedient or necessary; but when such cases do occur, the fervent priest will yield to them with reluctance, and will try to supply in some degree the omission by greater recollection and more frequent ejaculations than usual. But, after all, an essential distinction is to be made between an occasional omission and the habitual neglect of prayer: and, whatever may be said of the former in particular circumstances, it is certain that, with the latter, no priest, be his duties what they may, ought to consider himself in the secure way to salvation. The utmost concession which can be made with safety in favour of a Pastor, who is burthened with a very laborious charge, is, that he may abridge the time usually given by the fervent and pious to the exercise of meditation.

With regard to distractions, it is certain that they will be no prejudice to prayer, provided they be not wilful either in themselves or in their cause.—The state of spiritual dryness, too, to which the most perfect are liable, is generally permitted by the Almighty as a trial of a Christian's fidelity, or for his greater advancement in heroic virtues; and, when suffering under it, he should patiently and perseveringly do his best, leaving the rest to a kind and merciful God. To desist from prayer in the time of desolation is to lose all: whereas, by perseverance, he will deserve to find, and God in his own good time will show him, that He was not far off in his most trying moments of interior desolation. His duty is to humble himself before God; and, if he can say no more than the pious solitary, who in the state of dryness constantly cried out: "Thou who didst create me, have mercy on me," the time will be well spent. Moreover, to accept of dryness in the spirit of mortification and penance cannot but be most pleasing to God.

Finally, it is an error to suppose, that the spirit of prayer is above any person's reach. It is, on the contrary, adapted to every capacity, and human learning is of little assistance in the practice of mental prayer. By means of a single good thought a soul may, without mental exertion, unite itself to God in the most ardent and affectionate manner, and in this the value and perfection of prayer consists. By the help of a good will and the grace of God, mental prayer will become easy, as it will assuredly be of incalculable benefit, to all who apply themselves to it.

Third Day.

FIRST MEDITATION.

ON THE LOSS OF TIME.

Let us do good whilst we have time.—GAL. vi.

FIRST POINT.—Time is the price of eternity: nothing, consequently, can be more valuable. I shall be rewarded or punished after death, according to the good or bad use that I make of the time of this life; for, *each one*, says the Apostle, *shall receive according as he hath done in time* (2 Cor. v.). My salvation, therefore, depends upon time; and as God, in creating me, imposed upon me the obligation of labouring for my salvation, so he has given me an absolute command to spend my time well.

It was not for my sole advantage that God gave me my time; he had, also, his own glory in view, and to this he intended the employment of my time to be referred. To rob him of it, then, is a crime of similar character to that of a servant, who refuses to devote his time to the service of his master.

A material aggravation of this sin is that

time once lost cannot be recalled—it can never return. And, on the contrary, each day, hour, and moment of my life, if well spent, will increase my merit for eternity a hundred fold. But what fund of merit have I as yet accumulated? When the hour of death shall arrive, where shall I be able to look for the fruit of my past years? I shall then regret the mis-use of them; but all my regret will not recall them. I shall then see both what I might have gained, and what I have actually lost. I shall bitterly lament my fate; but my lamentations will terminate in this sad conviction, that my years are gone by and will never return:—that an immense gain was once within my reach, but is no longer so; that I might have escaped my present woeful fate, but cannot now. Oh! were I this day so happy as to conceive a true idea of the import which these words will bear at the hour of death—*I once might, but cannot now*—I should immediately have recourse to God, and resolve a thousand times to spend my future days more profitably than the past. These resolutions I will make at present, whilst they may be advantageous to me, and I have the opportunity of putting them in practice.

SECOND POINT.—A Pastor may lose his time, no less than another person; and when the necessary duties of his ministry do not engage the whole or much the greater part of it, he is perhaps more exposed to the danger of this misfortune than he would have been in another state of life. Many priests have not full employment for their time; and how do they dispose of that portion of it which the duties of their ministry leave unengaged? Are there none who spend much of it in useless company and conversation—in unnecessary visits—in curious inquiries into every thing that is passing—in meddling with affairs which do not concern them—in worldly business—in unprofitable reading—in immoderate re-creation, or even in some absolute trifle unbecoming the dignity and gravity of the sacerdotal character? For one engaged in the sacred ministry thus to squander away his time is a sin beyond comparison greater than that of an ordinary Christian, who passes his time unprofitably. How disedifying must it be in the eyes of the world, to see a priest devote any notable portion of his days to trifles! Does it not plainly indicate a disordered interior? Does it not give strong grounds for suspicion, that he is a stranger to the genuine spirit of the Ecclesiastical vocation, which should prompt him ever to have his Master's business uppermost in his mind, and his hands, consequently, engaged either directly or indirectly in something that will promote his Master's glory? No Pastor duly alive to the awful responsibilities of his state, will ever be at a loss for proper employment of his time. Where is the Pastor, even of the smallest flock, who can find none amongst them in need of his solicitude and attention? or who has not sufficient motives for prayer and study? Knowing, as I do, that I received my education, and was called to the priesthood, solely in order to labour for the salvation of souls,—and knowing also that I am accountable to God, not only for every soul under my charge that is lost, but for every privation of external grace which each one suffers through my neglect, I ought to tremble, lest any day or hour not given to my duty should be set down against me as time misspent.

It is not to be supposed, that Pastors more fully occupied with the indispensable duties of their vocation may not also lose their time. If they perform their duties with negligence —if they be impelled to them by human motives—if they regard them as an intolerable burthen, and hence show more solicitude to get them done than to do them well,—or, in short, if they have not purely in view the honour and glory of God, this is, at least, equivalent to a loss of time.

From these considerations I must infer, 1st, That, although there be no particular law commanding a specific employment of my vacant time, there is, nevertheless, a general law requiring it to be well spent;

and, consequently, that it would be sinful to consume the whole, or a considerable portion of it, in any of the unprofitable ways already mentioned.—2nd, That a very laborious life may be quite fruitless, if I attend to occupations of mere choice at the expense of any part of my duty.—And 3rd, That, in order to employ my time well, I must do all my duties from the motive of the will of God, and in order to please him. In examining myself by these rules, how much of my time shall I find to have been well employed? Can I make certain of a single day?

THIRD POINT.—Although time once lost never returns, still the loss is not altogether irreparable, for the Apostle exhorts me to *redeem the time* (Eph. v.); and I know that the labourers in the vineyard, who did not commence their work until the eleventh hour, received, through the generosity of the master, equal recompense with those who had begun to labour at earlier hours of the day. It is well for me that God is equally generous to me. But I should remember, that there is danger in every moment that I delay to avail myself of his call, because it is uncertain how soon *the day*, in my regard, may close. I know that, by the due employment of future time, I may compensate for the omissions of the past; but I am also aware, that nothing is more uncertain to me than the future. God grants me the present; but I cannot tell that he will grant me a future time. It is, therefore, a part of prudence, to turn each moment of the present to all possible advantage. Could I even make certain of many years to come, would it be too much to consecrate all to God, in compensation for what I have already mis-employed? I ought to be excited to activity and energy by the exhortation of my divine Master, to *walk whilst the light is, lest the night should overtake me* (John xii.).

CONCLUDING PRAYER.—O God of mercy! behold me humbled and prostrate before thee, like the servant who, being unable to discharge the debt which he owed to his master, moved him by the earnestness of his prayer to take compassion on him and forgive him. My lot is in thy hands: my days, I am aware, are numbered; but *have patience with me, O my God, and I will pay thee all* (John ix.). Yet a little more time, and I will do my utmost to make thee satisfaction.

My dearest, my eternal interests, O Lord, are at stake; and, if thou refuse the requested delay, I am undone. If thou call me now before thee, what a miserable appearance shall I make? The saints, I know, often prayed for the end of their banishment, and sighed with impatience after the eternal years to come. But they were saints; their days, consequently, were all full days, and, having grown rich in merit on earth, it only remained for them to be called to enjoy for ever the riches of thy glory. But, as for me, O Lord, I dread the end of my time, and I have reason to dread it. I have cause to tremble, lest death should quickly come and cut short those years, which I am sensible will be necessary that I may compensate for the bad employment of the years gone by. But, my God, I put my trust in thy Providence; yet so that I am determined not to tempt it by the loss of another moment. I will not delay until to-morrow. I begin to-day—this very instant. It is late, I own; but not too late, I hope, to serve thee and to sanctify my soul.

SECOND MEDITATION.

ON DEATH.

It is decreed for all men once to die.—HEB. ix.

FIRST POINT.—Nothing is more certain or more inevitable than death. It is a penalty to which the divine justice has condemned all mankind—a general law, from which there is no exception. Death consists in a total separation from all things here below, from goods, honours, pleasures, duties, and employments—from relations, friends, and acquaintance—and, in a word, from whatever constitutes the temporal life of man. The dead take no more part in the affairs of this life; they are neither seen nor heard, and are soon forgotten. These are considerations at which nature is apt to revolt, though of themselves they are only of minor consequence; and even as to the pain of dying—the pangs and agony of death, however violent they may be, are soon over.

It is the eternal consequence, then, of death, which renders it so truly formidable; for the moment of my death will be to me the commencement either of a happy or of a miserable eternity. The very instant in which it can be said of me with truth—*he is dead*—in the same it may with certainty be added—*he is judged—his lot is decreed before God—he is either lost or saved, chosen or rejected for ever.*

It is a great aggravation of the terror of death, that I have not, and cannot possibly acquire, any knowledge of the time, when this awful decision of my destiny to happiness or misery eternal will take place. Whilst nothing is more evident to me—nothing which I more freely acknowledge, than that I must die, nothing is more uncertain or more hidden from me than the time when. Not a day comes, that may not be my last; and, consequently, not a day, on which my fate may not be decided for endless ages.

These are useful and salutary reflections for persons of all states and conditions; yet for none more so than for me. But what effect have they hitherto had on me? What have I done, and what am I now doing, to prepare for death? Am I, at this moment, in a fit condition to appear before my sovereign Judge? Should I be content to die in my present state? I have only to consult my conscience impartially, and it will return me a faithful answer. What does it say? Does it make me no severe reproaches? Does it assure me that—certain allowances being made for the frailty of human nature—nothing essential yet remains to be done? These are matters which require my serious and unceasing attention. Knowing, as I do the infinite importance of dying well,—knowing that I may die at any hour,—and having reason to fear that I am not in those dispositions, in which I shall desire to be found at the hour of death, can further inducement be wanting to make me set about the work of preparation without delay?

SECOND POINT.—The last moments of all sinners, according to the assurance of the Spirit of God, are very evil. They are very evil because sinners then fall either into blindness and insensibility to the awfulness of their situation, or into despair of the divine mercy; and they are sovereignly evil from the state of final impenitence, wherein they are about to terminate. But the dying moments of a priest and Pastor, who has not lived up to his vocation, are still more sovereignly evil and deplorable. What alarm and terror must fill his breast on the bed of death, when, reviewing his past life, he perceives but too plainly that he has spent it in the omission of many essential duties!—That he has been living in the house of God without having made any progress in the ways of God!—That, although, in choosing the Lord for the portion of his inheritance, he had professed to renounce the world, still he has been all along as full of the spirit of the world—as fond of its vanities—as eager after all that it values and admires—and as destitute of the Spirit of God, as the generality of men!—That he has frequently neglected opportunities of promoting the glory of his heavenly Master and the good of souls!—And that he has consumed in vanity and sin hours, days, and years, which by prayer, study, and exhortation, he might have made available to the spiritual welfare of many—some of whom have already perished, others are in the way of perishing, eternally! Ah! then do *the sorrows of death encompass him, and the perils of hell find him.* (Ps. cxvii.) Then does he become sensible of the sinful attachment to life, to the world, and to himself, that holds him fast in chains, which he knows not how to break.

Has he recourse to God? Alas! the very thought of God is calculated to fill him with pain and desolation; for he is conscious how unfaithfully he has served Him, and, therefore, how unworthy he is of divine consolation. A thousand sins, which his sloth or indifference made him regard as trifles,—a thousand doubts, which in health he either would not take the necessary trouble to clear up, or erroneously decided in his own favour, —all now present themselves before him in quite different colours. Hence arise the most desolating doubts of the entire of his past performances, his confessions, his sacrifices, his administration of the sacraments, and his general dispositions. Hitherto his conscience had given him but little trouble on these heads; but being now rectified at the near prospect of death, it overwhelms him with alarm; for he knows that one mortal error neglected was sufficient to render the whole of his sacred duties a series of sacrileges and profanations. Whatever efforts he may make, or may be made by others, to excite him to confidence in the divine mercy, his mind still remains clouded with painful and restless uncertainty, because he is aware that that terrible truth, which his own lips have oftentimes announced, holds equally good with reference to a priest as to any other person, that—*as a man lives, so he dies.*

THIRD POINT.—As in the sacred text we are forewarned of the evil of a bad death, so God there assures us, that *the death of the just man is precious in his sight.* It is precious, because he dies in a holy disengagement from all earthly things;—precious, because he dies in a sweet and consoling confidence;—and precious above all, because he dies in friendship with his Creator. Such is, in a particular manner, the death of a faithful Minister of Jesus Christ. In his last moments the Almighty showers down upon him an abundance of his consolations, warning him that his labours are at an end, and holding out to him the crown of glory, to which they entitle him. All the merits of his laborious life are collected to his view, and the interior joy, with which the sight fills his soul, greatly assuages the pain of dying. Emboldened by the overflowing unction of divine grace, he not only consents, but even desires, to die. The union formed during life between God and his soul, becomes still more close and intimate in death. It costs him nothing to produce acts of all the great Christian virtues. At a word spoken to him of God and heavenly things, he forgets his bodily pains, and his heart becomes inflamed with holy desires. In short, when the moment pre-ordained by his heavenly Father arrives,—by a grace, which is the consummation of all other graces, he breathes out his soul in final perseverance, and passes to the eternal sight, enjoyment, and possession of his God.

CONCLUDING PRAYER. — Why, O Lord, should I deliberate a moment about the choice, which thou art now pleased to offer me, of making either a good or a bad death? I know that by choosing the former I must, at the same time, make choice of a holy life, because, in the ordinary decrees of thy Providence, thou dost not grant the one without the other; and that it would be vain to expect to die the death of the just, unless, like them, I serve thee faithfully during life. I am confident there is no exception in my favour from this general law. When, therefore, O God, will my coldness and indifference in thy service terminate? Make me sensible, at present, of my real state;—let the fear of death so operate upon me, that I may not have cause for serious alarm, when the moment of it shall be at hand.

In asking for the fear of death, I mean not that fear which proceeds from a love of life—that fear which induces so many to reject the thought of dying as an ungrateful alloy of their earthly enjoyments. No: a fear of this kind, I know, would not merely be useless, it would be prejudicial to me. What I pray for, O Lord, is such a fear as thou ever grantest to thy saints;—a fear which will keep my last end always present to my mind, and admonish me that, to die happily, I must live well. Give me a dread of the terrible consequences of a bad death, that I may guard against them, and labour to work out my salvation with fear and trembling. Happy is he, whom a fear like this preserves in a state of persevering watchfulness. May it please thy infinite mercy, O my God, to enable me to draw from it this fruit of grace and salvation.

THIRD MEDITATION.

ON JUDGMENT.

It is decreed for all men once to die, and after that judgment.—HEB. ix.

FIRST POINT.—Although, at the consummation of the world, all mankind will receive a final and solemn sentence from Jesus Christ, the great Judge of the living and the dead, yet, I am taught by a fundamental article of the Christian faith, that, at the very moment my soul shall have been separated from my body by death, it will appear before the tribunal of God, where a particular and secret Judgment will be passed upon it.

The soul does not require to be transported to a distance, in order to appear in the presence of God. Wherever a persons happens to die, there he instantly meets the Almighty dispenser of justice; for God is everywhere, and can everywhere equally exert his omnipotence. No sooner, then, shall I have breathed my last sigh and ceased to live, than I shall find myself surrounded with the majesty of the Deity, who will impress me with so lively a sense of his presence, that the sensations of holy Job will seem to be accomplished in me; for, like him, I shall feel myself cast on an ocean of boundless extent, the waves of which, swelling like huge mountains around me, will seem to burst over my head and engulph me in their womb. Thus will God, without the assistance of any other being, envelope and take entire possession of me.

Vain would be the thought of flight or escape; for, having once fallen into the hands of the living God, there will be no possibility of deliverance. I shall be alone with him, without the slightest hope of succour. But, could I summon all creatures to my aid, what would their united efforts avail against the mighty Lord of all? My friends gathered around my lifeless corpse will bathe it with their tears, and offer their vows and supplications to God for mercy in my behalf; but even these will be without effect, unless supported by the holiness and merits of my own past life. Hence, I may truly say, that the moment after death, I shall be entirely abandoned to God and myself;—to God, as the arbiter of my destiny, and who is on the point of deciding it,—and to myself, now completely naked and destitute of everything but my works, whereon to rest my hopes for eternity. Should I be found wanting in these, the deficiency cannot be supplied, and I am undone.

Oh! what value shall I, in that moment, set upon a virtuous life! If I have faithfully corresponded with my vocation, how clearly shall I comprehend its excellence! What confidence shall I derive from the recollection of my poverty of spirit, flight of the world, assiduity in prayer, mortification of my senses, and my exactitude in all, even the smallest, of my Christian and Pastoral duties! How shall I then rejoice, that I had courage to offer violence to myself for the purpose of conquering my corrupt inclinations—that my conduct was not influenced by worldly interest, or human respect—and that I disregarded the suggestions of passion and self-love! Such considerations as these will be all the support that I can possibly receive under the terrors of that Judgment, wherein I shall have no friend to plead my cause—not one word to say on my behalf.

If, on the contrary, in that hour my conscience be without this testimony—if, seeing myself in the power of that Almighty Being, who is about to judge me by the good or bad employment of my past years, I can look back on little else than sloth, negligence, and omission of essential duties in my two-fold character of a Christian and a Pastor, how desolate, how overwhelming will be my condition! Oh! how shall I desire to retrace my steps and return to life, in order to make better use of it! But no: this will not be allowed. In spite of my reluctance to advance towards God, I shall be compelled to present myself at his tribunal, and to give an account of my mis-spent life. Too late I shall find, that it was my duty to have thought of these things sooner, and to have taken measures accordingly. But, happily for me, I have yet the opportunity of doing it, though it may not continue long. Surely I am sensible, that to escape the evils which I shall then dread, is a duty worthy of all my present vigilance and precaution.

SECOND POINT.—At all earthly tribunals regular proceedings are instituted; certain forms of law are observed; and the judge does not pass sentence, until he has made a thorough investigation of the cause. The accused is interrogated and confronted with the witnesses against him, and, unless the proofs of guilt be clear and in accordance with all the prescribed forms of law, he is not convicted. Similar forms of justice will be observed by the great Judge towards me, and, with this view, I shall undergo an examination the most minute, but, at the same time, the most expeditious and satisfactory.

1st, This examination will be most *minute*.—In the entire course of my life, from the time of my coming to the use of reason until the moment of my death, I shall not have entertained a thought in my mind, conceived a desire in my heart, spoken a word, performed an action, or omitted a duty, which will not be noticed in this examination. Then (since the transgressions on all these heads are generally accompanied with circumstances either aggravating or diminishing their guilt) every motive, intention, or other incident, will be placed in the scales of justice, and accurately weighed. Having, moreover, had obligations as a man gifted with the light of nature, as a Christian owing obedience to the evangelical law, and as a priest bound to the performance of particular duties, I shall be interrogated with relation to each of them. The eye of God will discover the smallest imperfection, that may have glided into my most pious works; and, as he will give me full credit for whatever was meritorious, so he will suffer nothing to pass, which may have tarnished their purity and deteriorated their sanctity.

2d, This examination will, also, be most *expeditious*.—The utmost diligence in research and reflection would not now enable me to arrive at a clear and exact knowledge of my past life: I should even find myself at a loss to render minute account of the thoughts, words, and actions of a single day. But no sooner shall my soul become separated from my body, than my whole exterior and interior will instantly be laid open to my view by Him, before whose eyes I am ever present, and who is incapable of forgetfulness. A single ray of the light of the Divinity will unfold the most remote and hidden objects. These objects will be concentrated into one point, and yet each one will be presented before me as distinct from the rest as if it alone were under consideration. In one and the same instant, I shall behold them all, and, notwithstanding their countless number and variety, my soul, by virtue of its new powers of action, will clearly discern each particular.

3d, Hence this examination, grounded neither on reasonings nor conjectures, but on a simple and evident view of my case as it really is, will necessarily be also most *satisfactory* and convincing. It will, indeed, be

F

so clear, as not to leave the least room for dispute or denial. Ah! how many sins, now entirely forgotten, will then be brought to light? How plainly shall I then discover the false grounds of numberless excuses and pretended justifications of my present conduct? How many doubts and difficulties, which I now resolve in my own favour, will then be decided against me? How many virtues, which at present shine in the eyes of the world, and gain me the character of a good Pastor and a holy priest, will then appear to have sprung from self-interest, vanity, natural inclination, or perhaps even downright hypocrisy?

What a spectacle will these discoveries be to my astonished view! Whatever I may wish to allege in my own justification, my conscience, rising up in testimony against me and giving me the lie, will concur with God in wresting from my lips this short but sad confession: *I have sinned* (2 Kings, xii.). Why do I not candidly make this avowal now, whilst I can do it with benefit to myself? Why do I not prostrate myself before God with sincere sentiments of humility and repentance, that I may escape being compelled to do it at his tribunal with all the agonies of mortal despair?

THIRD POINT.—According to the result of this trial, God will pass upon me a sentence either of reprobation or of election. This sentence, although unattended with the publicity and formality of the last and general Judgment, will be equally authentic and irrevocable. What the Almighty shall then decree, either for my woe or beatitude, he will never reverse, because, being no longer *in the way*, my soul can neither gain an increase nor suffer a loss of grace. I shall then be beyond the term both of sin and of merit. It is therefore of the utmost consequence, that this sentence should be favourable.

How awful are these reflections! How is it possible that I should not always have had them so deeply engraven on my mind, that I could, under no circumstances, forget them? To be more sensible of them now, I have only to imagine myself, at this moment, before the throne of the divine justice, and that (my examination over) I hear God thundering forth against me that awful sentence: *depart from me, thou cursed* (Matt. xxv.). O what a thunderbolt! I must depart from my God! I must leave for ever the source of all good! My Father strikes me so completely with his curse, that henceforth it will never be in my power to appease him: no hope remains of my ever arriving at the possession of him! Was it for this that he separated me from the world, called me to the sublime dignity of the priesthood, and furnished me with so many means of sanctification? No: his desire was, to unite me to himself more intimately than other Christians: but I have forced him to dismiss me from his presence, and to pronounce against me the sentence of eternal divorce! He wished to rank me amongst the most distinguished of his elect, and I have compelled him to send me to dwell with the lowest grade of the damned! He designed to exalt me to one of the first places in his kingdom; and his justice now demands that he hurl me into the deepest abyss of hell!— Well will it be for me, if the consideration of these appalling truths induce me so to spend the remainder of my life, that they may not be verified in me at the hour of death.

It is only by a change of life that I can escape the curse reserved for the wicked, and merit a judgment of benediction; for there is a blessing in store for the just, and a special one for the faithful ministers of God. Instead of that awful sentence, which awaits a life of irregularity and sin, how delightful will it be to hear from the mouth of my sovereign Judge these consoling words: *well done, thou good and faithful servant: because thou hast been faithful over a few things, I will set thee over many: enter thou into the joy of thy Lord* (Mat. xxv.). Transported with ineffable sweetness and delight I shall then feel, that all which God required of me, and all that I did for him was nothing compared with the reward. I cannot, therefore, do too much in the service of a Master, who will not be less liberal in crowning my obedience and fidelity, than severe in punishing my negligence and sloth.

CONCLUDING PRAYER.—Great God, who with a look canst shake the pillars of the firmament and cause the earth to tremble! O God, infinitely holy and holiness itself, in whose sight the heavens themselves are not pure! How will a weak and sinful creature like me be able to endure thy presence at the hour of death? If thou examine with rigour and judge without mercy, a life, which in the eyes of men is most innocent and holy, will be found defective, for no one can say, that he is without sin and worthy of thy love. What, then, will become of me?

And yet, my God, thy holy word gives me to understand, that at the Judgment, which immediately follows death, impartial justice will preside to the total exclusion of that mercy, which is the sole foundation of my hope. Let me, then, prevail on thee, not to defer my judgment until that day, but to judge me now, whilst thou canst exercise in my favour the salutary judgments of a tender and merciful Father. Yes, my God, judge at present all my infidelities and crimes, for it is but just that I should suffer the punishment due to them : but, oh! do not defer my judgment for that hour, when thou wilt *rebuke me in thy indignation and chastise me in thy wrath* (Ps. vi.).

But thou shewest me still greater mercy than this, in offering to relinquish thy right to judge me, provided I now enter seriously into myself, and make what reparation I can to thy injured justice. These advantageous terms I accept with all my heart, and in compliance with them I will, during these days of retirement, cite myself before the tribunal of my own conscience; I will be my own accuser, and will give evidence against myself. Having made a diligent examination of my whole life, I will proportion my penance to the enormity of my guilt. With an unfeigned desire of making thee full satisfaction, I will chastise myself to the utmost extent that my weakness will endure. Nor shall this be all: I will regulate my life better for the future. I will neither allow myself any indulgence, nor tolerate the least sloth or wilful imperfection in the performance of any part of my duty to thee, to my neighbour, or to myself; that, when thou shalt call, there may be nothing to hinder my approach to thee, or to delay the attainment of the eternal beatitude, which thou hast prepared for me in heaven.

CONSIDERATION.

ON THE PRAYERS OF A PASTOR FOR HIS FLOCK, AND PARTICULARLY ON THE DIVINE OFFICE.

FIRST POINT.—As the princes of the earth receive through the hands of their ministers the complaints and petitions of their subjects, so, by the order of divine Providence, the Pastors of his Church are the principal medium of communication between himself and his creatures. One of the most essential duties, therefore, of a Pastor is, daily to present the wants and necessities of the faithful before the throne of God. This office he executes by Prayer and Sacrifice. Hence originated the Canonical Hours of prayer, and the singing or recital of the Divine Office, —a duty of which none can neglect either the whole or a notable part, without incurring the guilt of mortal sin. From this it follows, that I ought to consider my Office not only as a duty, which should have a preference before all human affairs, but as one of the first and most important of my sacred occupations. The Divine Office, being in a special manner the prayer of the Church, and being said in her name, and for her intentions, is of more avail with God than any private prayers. If I recite it well, it will tend greatly to my sanctification, and to draw down upon my people an abundance of blessings. If I recite it ill, I can be at no loss to account for any other disorder that may exist in my life, or for any want of success in my ministry.

If I unhappily carry about with me a heart ever grovelling upon the earth, and which reluctantly permits me to snatch a few moments from vain or frivolous occupations to honour God with my lips;—if I give but a cold, languid, and inattentive expression to the tender and divine sentiments of the royal penitent in the Psalms;—if in the discharge of a duty, which, when rightly performed, is declared by St. Ambrose to be capable of assuaging all the pains and solicitudes of my ministry, I seem only hastening to get rid of a perplexing and odious yoke:—what good can I expect such prayer to obtain either for myself or for those whose intercessor I am appointed? Am I not, in the sight of God, the guilty cause of his withholding those graces, which his Providence had decreed to grant only to my prayers? On the terrible day of his vengeance, will he not shew me, that hundreds of unfortunate souls would have done penance in sack-cloth and ashes, had my fervent prayers come in to second their good desires?

It is much to be feared, that the general

depravity of the Christian world, the laxity of morality and discipline, the decay of faith and piety among the faithful, and the many curses, which the Almighty has inflicted on his Church, are mainly to be attributed to the sloth of her Pastors and their neglect of the great duty of prayer. We weep not between the porch and the altar: our languid and often sullied vows and supplications reach not the throne of God, so as to move the bowels of his mercy : the Church possesses few of those sure, because fervent, mediators, who, like Moses, can speak with a holy liberty to the Lord, oppose the execution of his vengeance, and arrest his arm when on the point of striking his people. These considerations, equally as true as they are terrible, ought to convince me how necessary it is that I should be a man of prayer.

SECOND POINT.—On the other hand, what abundant blessings and graces descend upon those portions of the Church which God is pleased to bless with fervent Pastors. These holy men resemble the angels, whom Jacob, in his vision, saw descending and ascending the mysterious ladder. They descend to receive and take charge of the supplications of the people, and they ascend to go and present them at the foot of the eternal throne ; and they never present them in vain, for there is no good which the prayers and intercession of a pious priest are not capable of obtaining from God. When the Almighty had determined to punish the crimes of the Israelites in the desert, he conjured Moses and Aaron not to intercede in their behalf, but to suffer him to give vent to his just indignation, signifying thereby, that it would not be according to the economy of his Providence to resist the entreaties of the High Priest and the Mediator of his covenant.

So devoted were the Pastors of the primitive Church to the duty of prayer, that the different hours of the day were distinguished only by the stated times for reciting the Divine Office. And how copiously did the dew of heaven flow upon the Church in answer to those prayers! How beautiful were then the tents of Jacob! How delightful to behold those assemblies of priests and laity, a thousand times more brilliant by the fervent zeal, the innocence, the piety, and the charity, whereby all were united in one heart and one soul, than the Church of after times, though adorned with titles, dignities, and crowns! I clearly see how advantageous and how necessary for the common good, are the prayers of the Pastors of the Church, and, for my part, I am determined to be no longer remiss in the performance of this sacred duty. I will daily discharge, with all possible fidelity, the office of intercessor for my people, by fervently presenting their respective necessities before the throne of God. I will be particularly careful to have this in view when I say my Office.

THIRD POINT.—The recital of the Divine Office, like that of all other prayers, requires respect, attention, and devotion.—1st, *Respect* :—The heavenly spirits, when singing the praises of God, tremble before his divine Majesty ; and shall not I, who am but dust and ashes, tremble with awe and veneration ? A lively sense of the respect due to the infinite dignity of Him, whom I address in the hour of prayer, will cause me to pronounce the words of my Office fully and distinctly. To say it with indecent haste is a violation, not of one only, but of every requisite for good prayer. It is unworthy of God, and he and his angels abhor it ;—it is incompatible with attention, for the mind cannot accompany the frequent changes of sentiment which occur, more particularly in the Psalms; and it is destructive of devotion, for it is a mockery, which does not possess even the poor merit of the prayers of the Pharisees, which yet were rejected by Jesus Christ. By such prayer I cannot be said to honour God even with my lips ; where, then, must be my heart ? But, overwhelmed as I am by the interminable duties of an extensive ministry, how am I to find time to recite my Office slowly and distinctly ? by adopting and diligently observing a proper rule of life, founded on that spirit of retirement, flight of the world, and self denial, which become a true minister of God.—Another reflection not less certain than impressive is, that all those Pastors, whom God blesses with marked success in their labours, are, without exception, men of prayer—men who delight to walk in his presence, and whom it would consequently be a repugnance to suppose capable of addressing Him in a manner, in which they would be ashamed to speak even to the meanest of his creatures.

It behoves me to examine what my practice has been in this regard. Have I not been accustomed to say my Office too hastily? —with more haste even than I use in prayers which are not of obligation? And have I not reason to fear, that I have thereby deprived myself, and those committed to my care, of many graces, which more respectful prayer would have obtained? I am resolved to amend for the future. I will no longer forfeit the fruit of my daily prayers, by saying them in a hurried manner. The few minutes gained by the difference between saying them well and ill are not worth the sacrifice of so great a good. Whatever other benefit I may derive from my present Retreat, this at least shall, with the blessing of heaven, be one, that henceforth I will say my Office with all due respect.

2nd, *Attention :*—The Church, in imposing upon me the obligation of saying the Divine Office, certainly requires me to pay a reasonable homage to the divine Majesty. But what part can reason have in an action, to which it pays no attention ? Prayer is the elevation of the soul to God : when my soul ceases to be raised up to him, I cease to pray : consequently, the law, which requires me to pronounce the divine praises, obliges me likewise to do it with attention. From this I must conclude, that, if I give wilful cause to distraction, or do not endeavour to remove distractions when I perceive them, I do not fulfil my obligation. To avoid distraction, I ought to choose a suitable time and place for saying my Office, and never begin it without having previously placed myself in the presence of God, and banished, as much as possible, all solicitude either about temporal affairs, or even my external duties.—What precautions have I hitherto taken ? Have I not said my Office with wilful distractions—wilful, at least, in their cause, by entertaining a misplaced affection for some person or thing ?

3d, *Devotion :*—In the homage of a rational creature to its God, the heart as well as the mind must be employed : both must act in concert. The merit, in fact, of prayer consists essentially in the heart, without the concurrence of which, attention amounts only to pure speculation and mere lip-service. In order to excite myself to devotion, besides proposing to myself the general intentions of the Church, I should always have some particular object in my prayer. Having taken a review of my own necessities, or of the wants of the whole, or of a part, or even of some individual of my flock, I should say my Office with a lively faith and confidence in the efficacy of these prayers above all others. This practice, besides tending to excite my fervour and devotion, will be a powerful preventive of distractions. But, if I commence my Office without any fixed object for my prayer, it is but natural that both my mind and heart should remain inactive.—What has heretofore been my practice? Instead of aiming seriously at devotion, have I not often, perhaps even habitually, regarded my Office as a heavy burthen, and thought only of discharging it as soon as possible? "Alas!" (I may say with Augustine) "what will justify me before God, if my prayers themselves tend only to my severer condemnation?"

Fourth Day.

FIRST MEDITATION.

ON HELL.

Depart from me, ye cursed, into everlasting fire.—
MATT. xxv.

FIRST POINT.—God, whose nature is goodness, and who now makes his sun to rise equally upon the good and the bad,—that God, who, for the sake of sinners and of his very enemies, descended from his throne of glory, clothed himself with humanity and died upon a cross,—notwithstanding these and many other evident tokens of the most tender love for his creatures, will never cast one favourable look upon any of the reprobate, nor suffer the blood, which he shed so abundantly in his passion, to plead in their behalf. His mercy, which will be communicated without measure to the rest of his creatures, will be to all eternity totally inactive in regard to the damned. These miserable beings will send forth the most lamentable cries—they will be overwhelmed with desolation, and, according to the language of holy scripture, will shed torrents of tears. Yet, this avenging God will not arrest his mighty arm, nor for one moment suspend his strokes of wrath ; but as long as he shall be God, will behold millions of souls all created to his own image, marked with the seal of his divinity, and bearing the characters of his sacraments, suffering the most inexpressible torments, without feeling the slightest degree of compassion for them.— Were not this revealed by Him, who is truth itself, I could not believe it possible. But it is an article of the faith which I profess. Truly, a damned soul must be something most hideous, that the Almighty should thus eternally hate it, and close against it every avenue to grace and mercy !

But what is it which thus disfigures and makes a reprobate soul so abominable in the sight of God ? Ah ! it is sin,—mortal sin, which always lives in it, and which can never die. With this indelible stain it will to all eternity remain a just and necessary victim of God's inexorable wrath. During life, the cursed soul might, by renouncing sin, have effaced this odious stain ; for then its damnation, although begun, was not consummated. But at the moment of death—that fatal term, when the means of repentance cease and sin becomes irreparable—anticipated damnation was made complete, and received its final consummation. Mercy, heretofore so solicitous to seek and to pardon the sinner, is now cut off, without a chance of return; the perpetual presence of sin unrepented of will be an eternal bar to its operation. For ages without end, justice alone will act, justice will strike, and justice will take satisfaction for its injured rights. How blind and hardened must I be, if from these considerations I do not learn—1st, To dread falling into the hands of the living God: 2d, To dread sin still more, as the only thing which makes his justice terrible: and 3d, Not to despise the mercies of the Lord, whilst they are so liberally offered me, but to avail myself of them as the surest—the only screen against his vengeance.

SECOND POINT.—Another circumstance not less astonishing and frightful is, that souls created expressly to see, love, and possess God, will never see, love, or possess him in Hell; but, on the contrary, notwithstanding their natural impulse towards him as their first beginning, their last end, and the only centre of happiness and repose, will eternally hate him, eternally blaspheme his holy name, and eternally find in the knowledge, which they will ever retain of his infinite perfections, their most rigorous torment and the source of their despair.

Being, on the one hand, separated from God, and this so *violently*, that they will at every instant experience the sensation of being forcibly dragged from his bosom ;—so *entirely*, that all alliance between them and him will be dissolved ;—and so *permanently*, as to deprive them of all means and hope of being ever united to him hereafter :— and, on the other hand, being unceasingly occupied with the remembrance of God, as the great and only real good—as a good, which had been designed to fill the desires of their hearts and make them perfectly happy —as a good, the privation of which is the summit of their misery, and which they have forfeited for such empty trifles—as a good, in short, after which they will ever sigh by a necessity inseparable from their very existence, but which, by an unrelenting fate attached to their condition, they will never obtain :—ah ! the sense of all this will perpetually knaw their bowels, and make them the prey to the wildest paroxysms of fury and despair !

Thus will the reprobate in Hell, by a cruel contradiction of sentiments, unceasingly regret the loss of God, and still hold him in horror ; and the very inutility of their regrets and desires will render the torment of them the more insupportable. For what can be more cruelly tormenting than to be always desiring what can never be obtained, and to be ever holding in abhorrence what can never be cast off ? The reprobate soul will always be in quest of God, and will never find him ;

she will never consent to a separation from him, and to this she is for ever doomed.—Thus is she wretched in every way,—wretched in being abandoned by God, and more wretched still in being so sensible of the greatness of her loss:—wretched in having failed in her pretensions to the inheritance of the kingdom of heaven, and still more wretched in being necessitated always to sigh after that blessed abode:—wretched in venting continual imprecations against her God, and far more wretched because, in the midst of her imprecations and blasphemies, she feels the most irresistible impulse towards that supreme author of all good. But why cannot the unfortunate soul divest herself of the remembrance of God. Why not extricate herself from the attraction, which inclines her towards him? Why not shake off that longing desire, which rules and tyrannizes over her? Because this *pain of loss* is thé severest torment which the divine wrath has prepared for the damned; and could the soul discover a means of escaping it, Hell to her would be deprived of more than half its woe.

These considerations will surely convince me of the necessity of examining my present dispositions with reference to God.—Have I good reason to hope, that I am now united to him by grace? If so, I cannot sufficiently bless him, nor take too many precautions against losing this inestimable treasure.—Have I cause to fear, that sin has effected, or is likely to effect, a separation between God and me? This should excite me to use the most prompt and vigorous remedies and preservatives against sin; for the external loss of God, which the reprobate will sustain in Hell, will only be a continuance of what was begun in time.

Third Point.—The gospel furnishes another striking consideration on Hell, which is, that the souls of the damned, spiritual though they be, are affected and tormented by a material fire;—that this fire ever retains its activity without the smallest diminution, and yet receives no other aliment than the breath of an irritated God,—that this fire, acting, too, after the last day, upon the bodies of the damned, will burn without consuming them, and that these bodies, immortal in the midst of devouring flames, will be susceptible of no other sensation than the intolerable pain of burning; that there will not be a single moment in which this fire will not burn with all its intensity, nor in which both the souls and bodies of the damned will not be equally sensible of its rigour—and that, to all eternity, it will never be extinguished, nor will a period arrive when any one of the reprobate will be liberated from it. Thus, in one way or the other, will all creatures contribute to the glory of the Deity; and those, who would not do it by partaking of the magnificence of his rewards, will be compelled to do it by feeling the severity of his justice. He desired to reward them with a munificence worthy of himself; they rejected his offers, and he will punish them with torments which none but a God can inflict. Thus will his power and his greatness be manifested not less in Hell than in Heaven.

The human mind, equally incapable of comprehending either the attributes of God, or the infinite enormities of sin, will in vain reason and argue upon the difficulties which these awful truths involve. As a Christian, however, I am not permitted to call them in question; and it should suffice for me to know, upon the testimony of God's unerring word, that multitudes of angels and human souls are now feeling the weight of his irresistible arm. Serious and frequent meditation upon the consequences of these truths, is of far more importance to me than an attempt to unravel what is mysterious in them. These consequences regard me as much as, and perhaps more than, others, because I am a priest charged with the care of many souls besides my own. Being a creature of God, he had a right to call me to the state of responsibility in which I am engaged; but in doing so, he has communicated to me lights and graces proportioned to the magnitude of the burthen. I have only to correspond with these, and my salvation is as secure in the priesthood as it would have been in any other state. Still I must ever bear in mind, that where more has been given more will be required, and that my very character obliges me to aim at greater perfection in all virtues, than if I were only one of the common faithful. I must remember, that, with all the special graces granted to me, it is very easy for me to lose my soul;—that many priests, who for years have corresponded more faithfully than I have done with these graces, have, in just punishment of certain negligencies and infidelities, been permitted to fall into greater, and, in the end, have perished eternally;—and that I have no right to presume that, if I am equally remiss in my duties to God and my neighbour, I shall be more mercifully treated. In a word, I must remember well, that it is not given to me to know whether I am *worthy of love or hatred*, and that, in this condition of absolute uncertainty relative to my present and future state, my only just ground of hope consists in making every effort—flying every danger—clearing up every doubt and embarrassment of conscience—doing continual violence to my senses and inclinations—exerting all my zeal—sparing neither pains nor labour for the good of souls—and endeavouring to *work out my own salvation with fear and trembling.* Without all this, I may justly fear that the very means ordained by God for my salvation, and for exalting me to greater glory than other Christians, will be the ground of my damnation, and this in a tenfold degree of rigour.

CONCLUDING PRAYER.—O Lord, how magnificent art thou in thy mercies, but at the same time how terrible in thy chastisements! The more I reflect on the rigours of thy justice, the more I am impressed with horror; and the more I feel, also, that I am indebted to thy infinite goodness; for I cannot be ignorant of what I have deserved. Many and innumerable are the sins which I have committed, and yet, instead of hurling me into the bottomless abyss, thou hast restrained the arm of thy justice.

This, O my God, is a mercy, for which I owe thee a debt of eternal gratitude. The fire of Hell ought to enkindle in my heart the flames of divine charity. It ought to renew my fervour, excite me to vigilance, and support me in the practice of the most austere penance. It ought to make me patient under all the ills of life, constant and persevering in the duties of my laborious calling, and most zealous in whatever will advance thy glory and the salvation of souls. I pray, O God, that I may reap this benefit from the consideration of the torments from which thou hast hitherto preserved me, but which may yet be my doom, and which I cannot ultimately escape but by an inviolable fidelity to thee, and the practice of all the virtues required of me both as a Christian and a priest.

SECOND MEDITATION.

ON THE PARABLE OF THE PRODIGAL SON.

And rising up he went to his Father.—LUKE XV.

FIRST POINT.—The parable of the Prodigal Son was designed by Jesus Christ to be both a model of sincere repentance, and a pledge of the divine mercy to repentant sinners. A young man, led on by the natural impetuosity of his age, leaves his paternal home, and goes into a distant country, intending to live there at his ease and in the enjoyment of unrestrained liberty. Soon, however, does he discover the emptiness of all his visionary schemes of happiness, and sufficient cause to wish himself again under his Father's roof. The first thing that moves him to repentance is a sense of his present misery. A few months of licentiousness and dissipation have sufficed to exhaust the fortune which had been portioned out to him, and to reduce him to the most abject penury. Sharing, but a short time before, in all the plenty of his Father's house, he is now brought to the necessity of selling that liberty, which it had been the height of his ambition to enjoy, in order to procure subsistence. But the avaricious and unfeeling master, to whom he had sold himself, denies him even bread, and leaves him to allay the cravings of his hunger by sharing in the loathsome food, which it is his daily task to give to the vilest of animals. In this cheerless hour of adversity—a time so well calculated to bring him to his senses—he enters seriously into himself, and the first thought that strikes him is the comparative abundance and comfort enjoyed by his own Father's domestics.

Who can fail to recognise a striking similarity between the wretchedness of the Prodigal Son and that of every soul, which has lost its first fervour and fallen into the abyss of mortal sin ? In that far country, whither the poor sinner has unhappily wandered astray, and where he has soon dissipated all his accumulated treasures of grace and merit, he is miserable in the extreme. No longer does he feel a relish for retirement and prayer; and the timidity of conscience and Christian vigilance, which formerly influenced him, are extinct. Instead of enjoying the interior delights of a life of virtue, and feeding on the bread of angels in the house of his heavenly father, he sells himself to hard and cruel masters, the unlawful desires of his heart, and goes in search of the empty satisfactions that are to be found in creatures. But even these (many of them at least) are inaccessible to him, and what he can procure are far from satisfying the inward cravings of his soul!

Am not I this unhappy sinner? And if so, what shall I do? Ah! *how many hired servants in my Father's house abound with bread, and I here perish with hunger?* Yes, how many of the common faithful, even of those under my care, do I know, who in their communications with God enjoy the sweetest consolations, whilst I, in a much nearer affinity to God, experience no relish for piety —no affection or esteem for holy things? Happy, after all, am I, in not being altogether insensible of my misery. And shall I always continue in this state? Shall I never make a serious effort to extricate myself from it? Yes: *I will arise and will go to my Father.*

SECOND POINT.—Having considered and deplored his misery, the Prodigal proceeds to a more generous and perfect, because less interested, motive of repentance. He remembers the former tenderness and love of his parent, and the thought overwhelms him with confusion. Sensible of the baseness of his conduct, he dissembles to himself no part of the enormity of his crimes against one so deserving of his gratitude and love. He reproaches himself with his infidelities, and feels for them all that sorrow and regret which genuine repentance never fails to inspire. Penetrated with these feelings, he determines to return home without delay, and to make all possible satisfaction to his offended parent.

Before setting out on his journey, he considers and resolves what to say and do, when arrived in the presence of his Father. 1st, He determines to cast himself at his feet, there to acknowledge all his guilt—to pretend no excuses, but merely to declare the sincerity of his sorrow for his past misconduct; *I will say to him: father, I have sinned against heaven and before thee: against heaven*, by the violation of the divine precept of filial submission and obedience; and *before thee*, by my base ingratitude and contempt of thy salutary instructions and advice.—2d, He is induced by just indignation against himself to perform an act of still greater humiliation, by not pretending to the honour and happiness of being restored to his former rank amongst his father's children: *I no longer deserve to be called thy son;* not having behaved as a Son to thee, I cannot expect thee to treat me as a Father.—3d, He does not even stop at the humiliation of being degraded from the station to which his birth had entitled him, but purposes to ask for no other office or treatment in his Father's house, than that of a common menial: *reckon me as one of thy hired servants;* even this is more than I have a right to expect, and I shall be but too happy in being admitted under thy roof on these terms. O what language and dispositions are these in a young man, but a short time before so head-strong and presumptuous, so fond of his own ease, and addicted to sensual gratifications! What a change, what a conversion is this!

These sentiments, however, are only the necessary fruits of a solid conversion, and, if I have imitated the Prodigal in his wanderings, I am bound to adopt them as my own. Did the Father of the Prodigal Son ever do for him what can be compared with the favours and blessings for which I stand indebted to the Providence of my God? And would it not be the height of ingratitude in me to continue unmoved by the remembrance of all that he has done for me? If my contrition be sincere, it will produce these three effects:—

1st, It will cause me to return immediately to God, to cast myself with all humility at his feet, to acknowledge all the disorders of my life, to detest them from the bottom of my heart, and bitterly to bewail them. I have sinned, my God! yes, *I have sinned against heaven and before thee*, not once only, like the Prodigal Son, but my treasons have been repeated again and again! Far be it from me to pretend to extenuate my guilt by vain excuses: were I to attempt it, my heart would give me the lie, and the light of thy wisdom would confound me. No, my heavenly Father, I have no excuse to allege for my manifold sins; and, in order to excite thy compassion, all that I can do is, to make a sorrowful confession of them.

2d, It will unfold to me, amongst other motives, one which should induce me to despise myself and to hold my baseness in the greatest possible horror, viz., the opposition between my past life and the sanctity of my profession. Alas! I bear the character and have the name of a priest; but where are the signs of the true spirit of my vocation ? The name, which ought to be my glory, is my confusion. O my God! can I be surprised that I am not favoured with those choice graces and divine communications, which are the portion of thy faithful ministers ? Whilst I dishonour and refuse to obey thee as a Father, I cannot wonder that thou dost not treat me as thy child, and feed me with the bread of thy children.

3d, I shall determine to condemn myself to a life of severe and continual penance, so as neither to spare myself, nor wish that others should spare me ; cheerfully to accept all the difficulties, trials, and disagreeable occurrences attendant on my ministry ; and to be willing that God should suffer me to feel the whole weight of his burthen without alleviation or intermission. It is enough for me, O my God, that thou dost not altogether abandon me ; and I acknowledge that it would be just to treat a rebellious son like me rather as a mercenary and a slave, than with the endearments and indulgence, which a parent is wont to show towards a dutiful child. These are the sentiments, this the conduct of a soul that is truly contrite ; and they ought to be mine.

THIRD POINT.—With all his purposes of humble submission, the Prodigal does not know that, on his arrival in the presence of his father, he will meet with a favourable reception. On the contrary, a sense of his enormous guilt, and the horror which he knows his father cannot but entertain of his disorderly conduct, naturally tend to fill him with fear and distrust. But he reflects that he is going to one who is, and who cannot divest himself of the remembrance that he is, his father : and the very name of *Father* inspires him with a confidence, which banishes all further deliberation.

Thus supported and encouraged under his

fears, he sets out on his journey, and, before reaching its termination, his hopes of obtaining forgiveness are more than realized.— Whilst he is yet afar off, his father sees him coming, and, without a moment's delay, rushes out to meet him, throws his arms about his neck, and gives him the kiss of peace. He introduces him once more under his roof, and, without so much as adverting to his misconduct, assembles the whole family to testify to them, and make them partakers of his joy. Nor is this all: so far from treating this spendthrift and Prodigal Son as a mercenary or a slave, he clothes him with a new robe, orders the fatted calf to be killed and a feast to be prepared, *because*, says this tender father, *this my son was dead and is come to life ; he was lost and is found.*

The same indulgent reception does the sinner meet with, who returns sincerely to Almighty God. If I go to him with sentiments of true compunction, and, from an inward conviction of my unworthiness and infidelities, humble myself before him, I shall find him equally as well disposed to receive me, as was this father to receive his Prodigal Son. It is true that, consistently with the rules of strict justice, God might reject me ; but his goodness is the foundation of my confidence ; so that, if I do my best to satisfy his justice, I cannot doubt but the immeasurable treasures of his mercy will be opened to me. Away, then, with all the doubts and fears which nature would inspire and the enemies of my salvation would suggest, to keep me back. Whatever repugnance I may feel, a genuine spirit of penance will determine me to overcome it. Nay, the moment that I set out in earnest to seek the Almighty, I shall discover how futile are the fears and how false the alarms created by the sight of my disorders and frailty. Instead of a severe and inexorable judge, I shall find the Almighty a Father full of tenderness and compassion.

However grievous, therefore, may be my offences, and whatever cause I may have given God to banish me for ever from his face, I may be assured, 1st, That he will come forth to meet me in order to facilitate my return:—2d, That he will grant me a speedy remission of all my sins:—3d, That, in order to my thorough conversion and perseverance, he will strengthen me with his grace:—4th, That he will lead me on in the paths of perfection, so that nothing but my own fault will prevent me from regaining all that I have lost:—and 5th, That, without my seeking for them, he will shower down upon me such heavenly consolations, as will prove an ample indemnity for all the sacrifices that I am required to make. What more than this can

I desire? And why should I hesitate a moment about coming to a decision? *I will arise*, then, *and will return to my Father.*

CONCLUDING PRAYER.—Blessed be thou, O Father of mercies and God of all hope and peace, for the holy resolution with which thou hast inspired me. Confirm it, I beseech thee, by a continuance of thy grace. Filled with confusion at the sight of my miseries, I cast myself at thy feet with an assured confidence in thy paternal goodness. I hear thy voice inviting me to return to thee; how, then, can I fear that thou wilt reject me?

I know, O Lord, that all I can do would be nothing, were thou to treat me with the strict rigour of thy justice, for *what is man to be able to answer God?* (Job vi.) But I have a resource in thy paternal goodness, and no one shall rob me of the confidence which I repose in it. No, my God, that confidence, which has supported so many other penitents, shall be my guide and support. It shall stimulate me to an attentive performance of all my duties, and to do them through the motive of gratitude and love. Far, however, from letting my confidence in thee serve as a pretext for sparing myself the rigours of a penitential life, the more sensible I become of thy clemency, the more clearly I hope also to comprehend the injustice and grievousness of my crimes, and the necessity of making all possible satisfaction for them by a life of penance. Accept, O Lord, and assist my feeble efforts. Look down with a favourable eye upon my good will and sincere intentions. I set out towards thee: do thou meet me on the way. Let such a reconciliation be established between us as will last through time and eternity.

THIRD MEDITATION.

ON THE REIGN OF JESUS CHRIST IN THE SOUL OF A PASTOR.

Take my yoke upon you, and you shall find rest for your souls.—MAT. xi.

FIRST POINT.— To effect a sincere and lasting return to Almighty God after sin, it is necessary that the Reign of Jesus Christ should be well established in my soul. This Reign consists in renouncing every other spirit but his; in ever forming my judgment of things according to his maxims; in loving nothing which is not agreeable to him; and in copying so faithfully all his virtues in my life, that he may be said to rule and govern me, and to be the end of all my actions.

Unlike the kingdoms of the earth, whose monarchs rule in pomp and splendour, and

THIRD MEDITATION. 115

extend their conquests by force of arms, the Reign of Jesus is in poverty, obscurity, and humility, and his victories are gained by the sweet attractions which his own practice and example have conferred upon these lowly virtues. A soul, seeing her Head and Master walking before her in the thorny and narrow way, and feeling an inward impulse to follow him, yields herself up without reserve to his guidance. In whatever direction he is pleased to call, she follows him with courage and perseverance. To her his example is a precept, and whilst she beholds her Master teaching her how to surmount her difficulties, she would be ashamed to let them retard her progress. Like St. Thomas she generously cries out, *let us go and die with him* (John xi.). She remembers, *that the slave is not above his master* (Mat. x.), and, of course, that the creature is not above its God. He therefore becomes her guide in all her ways; —He gives impulse to all her motions;— he is the main-spring of all her actions, and her support under all her trials. Thus her submission is unreserved—her dependence is entire.

To conduct me to this state of subjection is the object of that precept of my divine Saviour: *take my yoke upon you* (Matt. xi.): a precept addressed to every Christian, but much more particularly to me, as a Pastor of souls. By the very nature of my vocation I am, to a certain extent, necessarily burthened with this yoke, which, although agreeable in itself, will be insupportable, if I attempt to carry at the same time the opposite yoke of the world. Two yokes are more than I can bear, and that of Jesus Christ will only be felt light and sweet in proportion to the perfection with which it is embraced, and that of the world rejected.

This, then, is the true secret of the art of attaining the perfection, to which as a priest I am obliged to aspire. I must allow Jesus Christ to reign in me, and I must not suffer his dominion to be controlled or divided by any other power. Hence, instead of gratifying, I must courageously resist, the evil desires of my heart, and combat all my natural inclinations;—instead of being in love with riches, I must renounce them, if not in effect, at least in affection, so as to be quite willing to share in all the hardships of the poverty of Jesus Christ;—instead of pursuing vain and ambitious projects, I must, like my Master, delight in humiliation and obscurity. And yet, is not the pursuit of the former of the two rival principles the slavery in which I have passed my days? Instead of cheerfully taking up the yoke of Christ, have I not ever been studying also to serve those hard masters that are never satisfied, sensuality and self-love? If so, can I be surprised at my past errors, or wonder that I experience not the unction and consolation, which Jesus has promised shall, even in this life, assuage the burthens of his faithful servants?

Ah! it is time that I should make room for the reign of Jesus Christ in my soul, and suffer him to establish a perfect dominion over me. There is no better Master—none more wise or more enlightened. He is *the wisdom of God (1 Cor. i.)*, and *has the words of eternal life* (John vi.). He requires nothing of me but what is both holy and reasonable in itself, and useful and salutary to me: nay, more, he requires nothing that he has not practised himself. Surely, then, I ought not be ashamed, or think it too hard, to follow the footsteps of my Saviour, to act with him and under him, to love what he loved, and to do what he did.

SECOND POINT.—There is a general law obliging all men without exception to submit to the dominion of Jesus Christ. The very laws of Christianity contain an universal command to take up the yoke of this Man-God, our legislator and our Master. To be, or rather to call ourselves, Christians, and yet to refuse to be ruled by Jesus Christ—to profess to be his disciples, and still to decline receiving his orders for the regulation of our actions and deportment—is a contradiction.

What was the object of our baptismal vows

and renunciations? Was it not to signify, that we would never submit to be the slaves of the enemies of Jesus Christ, nor yield to any other empire than his? Did we not at the sacred font put on his livery, and make a solemn profession at the foot of his altar, that we dedicated ourselves to him, and would ever obey his law? Moreover, faith teaches us, that we are the members of Christ, and that he is our Head,—that we are his flock and he is our shepherd,—that we are his Church, and he our high-priest,—that we are his people, the fruit of his conquest and the price of his blood, and that, by all these titles, he has incontestable dominion over us. In consequence of these common and general reasons, I can never without injustice swerve from an inviolable attachment and entire obedience to my divine Master. When he speaks, my duty is to listen; when he commands, it is for me to obey. His Gospel is his word: it contains his sacred commands and ordinances. To refuse, therefore, to obey it, would be the crime of rebellion;—it would be renouncing my baptismal engagements, and a species of apostasy.

But as a priest I am dedicated to Jesus Christ by a still more sacred obligation. I am appointed as a captain and leader in his army—a Pastor over his flock—a physician with heavenly medicines to heal their wounds and disorders. He has made me a mediator between himself and his people, and has placed in my hands the sacred victim, whereby heaven is propitiated. He has set me up as a light, which, by reflecting his own bright rays, may expose to public view the delusions of a benighted world, and exhibit to its wretched votaries the means of extricating themselves from its dominion. If, then, the want of attachment to his holy laws, even in a simple Christian, be so great a crime, where shall I find words adequate to express my own perfidiousness, should I refuse to allow him to reign in me and over me without control? A true sense of the sublime dignity to which I have been raised will never suffer me to be content, until I am dead to the world and live only to God— until I can say in the words of the Apostle, and with all his sincerity, *I live now, not I, but Christ liveth in me* (Galat. ii.), and in this life exhibit to men the emptiness of all their grovelling pursuits, and the value which they ought to set upon poverty, humiliations, and sufferings. Had I the happiness to live such a life as this, how much more abundant than it is would be the fruit of my ministry! how earnestly would my flock crowd around me to hear the voice of their shepherd! how eagerly would the ignorant press for instruction! how anxiously would the sick and infirm come to me for the cure of their spiritual maladies! and what an object of complacency in the sight of heaven, and of edification to the world, would be my little portion of the fold of Jesus Christ!

THIRD POINT.—It is an error to suppose, that the Reign of Jesus Christ in the soul is a heavy burthen or an intolerable yoke. To judge, indeed, solely by appearances, it might be taken for a condition of miserable slavery; but experience proves it to be a state favoured with the enjoyment of the happy liberty of the children of God and of unalterable repose. Still it is a burthen and a yoke: but then they are those of the Lord, and he has assured us, that his *yoke is sweet* and his *burthen light* (Mat. xi.). Yes: the spirit of interior and exterior mortification, the disengagement of the heart from all human ties, the total resignation to the appointments of Providence, the zeal for the glory of God and the relish for labour, which Jesus establishes in the soul wherein he reigns, are ever accompanied by that testimony of a good conscience, that inward peace, and those other secret communications of the Holy Spirit, which fill it with a joy most pure and divine, and abundantly compensate for all it has forsaken either in affection or in effect, and, in short, for anything it could possibly have hoped to possess in the service of the world.

Does not my own experience bear testimony to these truths? When I first entered upon the duties of the sacred ministry, I was less sparing of my labours, I lived more regularly, and accomplished the obligations of my state with more zeal and ardour than at present. And was not I at that time more happy and content than now ? Did I then find the yoke of my Master too fatiguing ? On the contrary, did I not experience under it a degree of sweetness and pleasure, which compensated for the violence that it required me to offer to human nature ? I then thought myself happy, and was really so. And when did I begin to experience a diminution of my happiness ? Alas! it gradually decreased as my zeal and ardour cooled—as I yielded to the demands of slothful nature, and withdrew myself from the dominion of my heavenly Master. My evil inclinations put in their claims, and I indulged them; my passions were excited, and I did not curb them; and, on numberless occasions, I have found that it would have been beyond comparison more conducive to my happiness and comfort, had I never deviated from the way of the Lord, or violated the severe maxims of his Gospel.

Being convinced of these truths, I cannot hesitate in the choice of my future course. If I design to recover the happiness which I have lost, I must dedicate myself anew to Jesus Christ, so that he may be the soul of my soul, and the main-spring of all my actions. Such a life as this, being a certain pledge of an eternal recompense in the life to come, cannot be too highly prized. The main design of Jesus Christ in wishing to reign in my heart at present is, that I may hereafter reign with him, and become a partaker of his glory. Had I nothing to hope for in this world, the immortal crown prepared for me in the world to come will surely be an abundant reward for all my services.

CONCLUDING PRAYER.—Come, O Lord, and take possession of this heart of mine, which by so many titles belongs to thee. Banish from it whatever keeps thee at a distance from me, and me from thee. Thou art a jealous God, who wilt admit no rival; and thou hast declared in thy Gospel that *no one can serve two masters.* If I must make choice of one, which can I choose before thee? or which shall I not renounce for thy sake?

Already have I chosen thee, O Lord, for the portion of my inheritance; and I am sorry that I have not always remained faithful to that happy choice. But I now, with all my heart, renew it, and with the humility, confusion, and sincere repentance of thy Apostle, I adopt his language as my own, and say to thee: *my Lord and my God* (John xx.). Command what thou pleasest, for I am ready to obey thee in all things. However hard and humiliating may be the way, which thou shalt point out, I will follow it. Call me, and I will answer; inspire me, and I will act; make known to me thy blessed will, and I will accomplish it. I will do all for the love of thee, who art the God of love, and by love reignest and exercisest sovereign dominion in the hearts of thy faithful.

CONSIDERATION.

ON THE SACRIFICE OF THE MASS.

FIRST POINT.—The peculiar office of the Priesthood of the New Law is to offer the holy Sacrifice of the Mass. At the Altar a Priest acts in the name of Jesus Christ, who, having once offered himself a bleeding victim of adoration, thanksgiving, propitiation, and impetration to his eternal Father, commissioned his Priests to perpetuate the same oblation, in an unbloody manner, until the end of time.

Great is the sanctity required in me for the due discharge of this august function. *Holy things are for holy persons.* Jesus Christ is present upon the Altar: his body, his blood, his soul, and his divinity are there. Although he be concealed from my corporeal senses, I am by faith as certain of his real presence as if, instead of the sacramental species, I beheld him in the effulgence of his glory. If, therefore, knowing him, as I do, to be the Lord of Glory, I presume to touch him with unholy hands, and to receive him into a polluted breast, I defile the blood of the sanctuary, and commit treason against the divine Majesty : my crime equals the crime of the apostate Judas and the outrages of the hardened Jews; for, like the former, I betray the Son of Man with a kiss, and, like the latter, as far as lies in my power, I renew upon his sacred person all the horrors of his passion and death.

Did no other motive exist, this consideration alone is sufficient to convince me of the necessity of ever keeping my soul and body free from all the defilements of sin, and of aspiring to a life of angelic purity and sanctity. One sacrilegious celebration would be a heinous crime, and might decide my doom to eternal reprobation. But, if I dare once to touch with guilty hands this Holy of Holies, it is more than probable that my sacrilegious impiety will not stop there, but will lead me into the same crime again and again. I may, indeed, seek refuge in my Saviour's wounds (those sacred wounds, which my own daring and impious act has caused to stream afresh), but, will the tears, which I shall then shed, spring from a truly contrite heart ? or, will they not be the effusions of mere anguish and remorse of soul bordering upon despair at the thought of having perpetrated a crime so hellish? Ah! I see plainly that I have no other security against the continual commission of the most grievous and revolting sacrileges, but by walking with undeviating constancy in the paths of holiness, and living in the habitual fear of having my soul defiled with the smallest stain of guilt.

Ever to live, therefore, in the state of grace is the first and most indispensable, but should not be the only, preparation for celebrating the tremendous mysteries. A lively sense of what I then perform, and of what I also receive into my breast, will convince me, that actual devotion ought always to precede my approach to the Altar. Before retiring to rest in the evening, I shall be careful to entertain myself, if only for a few moments, with reflections on what I am about to perform on the ensuing morning; and, when the morning comes, my waking thoughts and aspirations will be directed to my heavenly Spouse. Then, rising with alacrity, I shall set about adorning with acts of all the necessary virtues the habitation wherein he is to dwell. I shall, also, direct my devotion to the four great ends of sacrifice and the commemoration of the sufferings and death of my Redeemer, and form in my mind the particular intention, for which I am about to celebrate. In a word, until the hour of Mass shall arrive, I shall keep myself, as much as possible, apart from every external cause of distraction. Woe to me, if I am accustomed to go to the Altar without due preparation. Woe to me, if familiarity with holy things has rendered me almost insensible of their holiness. What has my practice hitherto been relatively as well to my remote as to my immediate preparation for the holy Mass?

SECOND POINT.—Nothing gives so much honour and glory to God, and so powerfully inclines him to shower down his blessings upon his creatures, as the Sacrifice of the body and blood of his Son; for the Almighty ever looks with complacency on the face of his Christ. The chief end of my ordination was to offer this sacrifice; and, from my appointment as a dispenser of the mysteries of God, I should be wanting in an essential point of duty to him, to myself, and to all entrusted to my spiritual jurisdiction and care, were I to neglect frequently to make this sacred oblation. I must not, therefore, imagine that I do my duty by celebrating the holy Mysteries on those days only, on which the faithful are commanded to assist at them. This opinion is as false as it is at variance with the practice of all zealous Pastors and truly apostolic men, who, sensible of the great injury daily offered to the divine

Majesty, and the heavy debt continually accumulating to his justice by the sins of their people, seldom omit, unless compelled by necessity, to celebrate Mass every day. I ought to propose these good Pastors to myself as models for my imitation; at least, so far as never to allow either sloth, mere worldly occupations or pleasure to be an obstacle to my saying Mass.

Whatever is connected with this most sacred and solemn action demands attention. Like the pious Psalmist, I ought to be in *love with the beauty of the house of God, and the place where his glory dwells* (Ps. xxv.); and be filled with zeal for whatever may contribute to the splendour and dignity of the divine worship. This love and zeal will cause me studiously to avoid the disgraceful and sinful carelessness of too many, who, whilst they observe the extreme of nicety in the decoration of their dwellings and the neatness of their furniture, pay not that regard to the cleanliness of the house of God, of the sacred vessels, of the altar linen, and of the other things appertaining to the adorable Sacrifice, which common decency requires. I shall be careful, likewise, to perform the ceremonies of Mass with suitable dignity, to pronounce the words with distinctness and gravity, and to observe with scrupulous exactness every tittle of the Rubrics, being ever fearful lest, by any outward signs of levity, haste, or other disrespect, I should shock the piety of the faithful, or give the libertine occasion to scoff at the holy Mysteries.

This external reverence will, in fact, be a necessary accompaniment of the inward veneration, which I am bound still more studiously to cultivate for Jesus Christ truly present upon the Altar. Hence, so far from giving occasion to, or wilfully entertaining, any distraction, I ought to be lost in admiration of the unspeakable condescension of Him, who has admitted me to an office, of which the angels are not worthy, and to endeavour to produce in my soul sentiments and acts corresponding with the sense of the words which I pronounce. I ought to be filled with humility, fear, and veneration, at the thought of my standing so near to Jesus Christ, and being permitted to behold him, as it were, face to face; and my soul should, at the same time, melt away with the tenderest affections of divine love at the prodigy of love, whereby Jesus Christ unites himself to me, and makes me a partaker of his choicest blessings. Such ought to be my conduct and devotion whilst saying Mass; but have I no cause to reproach myself with neglect on any of these heads? I will now examine myself impartially, and with the sincere desire and determination to reform whatever I may find to be defective.

THIRD POINT.—On leaving the Altar, it

would ill become me to retire immediately from the house of God, and devote myself to secular occupations. I should allow time for the heavenly Manna to digest and diffuse its virtues through all the powers of my soul. Whilst the food is in my mouth, it would be shameful to forget the hand that fed me.— Kneeling down, therefore, with all humility, and with a lively faith contemplating Jesus truly present within me and surrounded by the choirs of heavenly spirits, I should join with them in acts of adoration, love, and praise, and make an oblation of my whole soul and body to him, who has given himself to me. I should then lay before him all my spiritual necessities, and pour forth earnest supplications for all, in whose behalf I am bound to pray, not forgetting to make special intercession for those individuals whose spiritual wants are more particularly urgent.— Then, also, is the time for forming good and earnest resolutions, to banish from my heart whatever I can therein discover offensive to the eyes of infinite sanctity. I should not, in short, consider the precious moments, during which it is probable that Jesus Christ remains corporally present within my breast, too long to be entirely devoted to him; but endeavour so to entertain him, that I may reasonably hope that, on his departure, he will leave a copious blessing with me and mine.

But, what use have I hitherto made of this bread of life in the Holy Eucharist? What has been my usual devotion after saying Mass? Have not very trifling occurrences frequently caused me to abridge or omit my thanksgiving? Where are the fruits of all my Sacrifices? Have I grown proportionably stronger in virtue, by having fed so often, perhaps for many years, on the bread of angels? Do I gain a daily increase of fervour, such as the holy Sacrament necessarily produces where it meets with no obstacle to its operations? Do the frequent communications, which Jesus Christ makes of himself to me, draw me to a more intimate union with him, and to a more perfect resemblance to him in humility, contempt of the world, zeal, charity, and every other sacerdotal and Christian virtue? Am I not, on the contrary, less filled with veneration for the tremendous Mysteries, and in every respect less perfect, than when I was ordained to the Priesthood? Has not my approach to the Altar become a mere act of habit and custom? and are not my numberless negligences, faults, and omissions in every part of my duty relating to it, so many proofs of great coldness, indifference, and insensibility? Oh! if my conscience cannot return a favourable answer to these interrogations, I have the strongest reason to fear, that this celestial food has, by my own neglect and unworthiness, not merely failed in the effects which it ought to have produced, but has actually been converted into a mortal poison.

Fifth Day.

FIRST MEDITATION.

ON THE HUMILITY OF JESUS CHRIST IN HIS INCARNATION.

He annihilated himself.—PHIL. ii.

FIRST POINT.—The Incarnation of the Eternal Word is a mystery, of which no just idea could be conveyed to our minds but by the spirit of God himself, who has admirably expressed the wonders which it contains in these words of the Apostle: *he annihilated himself.* This is the great secret hidden in God from all eternity, and revealed to us in time. Yes: the Incarnation of the Word is truly the annihilation of God, who thereby condescended to unite himself in one individual person to what was before at an infinite distance from him. After the serious contemplation of this, no other mystery in the life of Jesus Christ can appear astonishing. For, to embrace poverty, contempt, sufferings, and the cross, is but the natural consequence of his having assumed human nature. For God to become man was a step, to which he could have no other inducement than his boundless charity. Were a man to descend to the condition of a contemptible insect, he might be said to have stooped to a sort of annihilation; and yet this is nothing when compared to the annihilation of an Incarnate God. For, between man and the vilest insect there is some proportion: whereas, between God and man there neither is nor ever can be any.

The Scripture, moreover, informs us, that the Son of God assumed to his divine nature that which is most mean and lowly in man, namely, our flesh: *the Word was made flesh* (John i.),—that flesh, which is so despicable in itself, subject to so many infirmities, and is withal common to us and the very brutes. Again, in becoming man, he might have exempted himself from passing through the helpless state of infancy, and appeared upon earth in the maturity of manhood, like the first of the human race. But no: he chose to be conceived in the womb of a Virgin, to remain there like others for the space of nine months, to be born, and to proceed through the humiliating stages of infancy, childhood, and youth. Besides, he might have been born of some prince or monarch of the earth; but he preferred to come amongst us in a state of the most abject dependence, *taking*, as the Apostle says, *the form of a slave* (Phil. ii.), in order to reduce himself to the lowest possible condition of Humility and abjection. Oh! what an inconceivable mystery that the Lord and Master of the universe should stoop so low!

But, is it not almost equally inconceivable and incredible that, with such an example before my eyes, any particle of pride should either appear in my deportment or reign in my heart? And yet I feel the most trifling humiliation—I am displeased at the least offensive word—I cannot bear reproof—I am hurt to see others preferred before me—I am so desirous of notice and esteem, that I envy a fellow-labourer, who is more successful than myself—nay, so full am I of myself, that if I saw a probability of success, my ambition would prompt me to aspire to offices of trust and dignity. *Dust and ashes, why art thou proud?* (Eccles. x.) How forcibly does this reproach apply to me, who, as a Christian, am obliged to worship an annihilated God! But, how much more applicable is it to me as a priest, in which character I am bound to aim at the most perfect imitation of my Master, both in my sentiments and my conduct! And yet, alas! the dignity to which I have been elevated, so far from inspiring me with true sentiments of Humility, tends only to puff me up with vanity, and to remove me farther from a resemblance to Jesus Christ, than if I had remained in the ranks of the common faithful!

SECOND POINT.—The annihilation of the divine Word procured the greatest honour to God; for by it the glory of the Deity was repaired, and man was redeemed. On it is founded our justification, and through it we are enriched with the treasures of God's infinite mercy. Hence has this abjection of Jesus Christ been more glorious to the Almighty, more salutary to men, and in every respect more beneficial, than if he had come amongst us in majesty and splendour. O infinite power of the Most High! O abyss of wisdom! How adorable art thou, O Lord, in all thy counsels!

Similar effects, in a certain degree, will be the fruit of humility in me. Whatever may be the designs of God in my regard, and whatever good he may intend to produce through me, I may be quite certain, that its foundation must be laid in my Humility. If I pretend to be any thing, I am nothing; but the moment I descend into the abyss of my own nothingness, I become a fit instrument in the hands of God for doing the greatest things. The most strenuous labours, supported by the brightest talents and most extensive acquirements, will be all in vain, if through pride I place any part of my dependence upon them, instead of God alone. Humility was the groundwork of the perfection of all the saints, and without it there can be no genuine sanctity. The body of my actions may be the same as those of the saints; but, if the spirit of my performances be infected by pride, they are dead works; and, whilst their eternal splendour dazzles the eyes of men, their inward deformity makes them detestable in the sight of God.

Of what value, in fact, can I suppose those works to be with God, which are done, not for his sake, but to gratify my own vanity, and to attract the notice and esteem of others? Even if I do not go so far as formally to seek myself, but really think that I have God in view, the merit of my performances will be destroyed, if I attempt to divide the glory of them with him by taking pleasure in the commendations of men, and dwelling with complacency on what I do. It is easy for pride to assume the mask of Humility. I must, therefore, be ever upon my guard, and remember that He, who is jealous of his own glory and will not suffer me to rob him of the smallest portion of it, sees the inward motions of my heart.

In accordance with these maxims we find, that when the Almighty pleases to raise up models of extraordinary sanctity in his Church, or to employ creatures as instruments in the execution of any great design, he invariably selects the most humble. She, who was elevated to the divine maternity, was the most humble of virgins. Through the instrumentality of poor fishermen, the gospel was proclaimed and the Church founded. How admirably has St. Paul declared this truth where he says,—*for you see, brethren, your vocation, that there are not many wise according to the flesh, nor many mighty, nor many noble. But the foolish things of the world hath God chosen, that he may confound the wise; and the weak things of the world hath God chosen, that he may confound the strong; and the base things of the world and the things that are contemptible hath God chosen, and the things that are not, that he might bring to naught the things that are, that no flesh should glory in his sight* (1 Cor. i.).

On the other hand, numberless examples occur of the severest judgments exercised upon those presumptuous beings, who allow themselves to be puffed up with their pretended merits. Nothing is more common than for the Almighty to permit men, and those even who are apparently doing much good, to fall into very shameful disorders in punishment of pride. If his severity has not extended so far with me, is it not still a deplorable misfortune that I should lose, through empty pride and ostentation, the merit of my sacred performances and of all my labours for the salvation of souls? What a sad thing it will be, if, after having sunk under the weight of years and been worn out with labour, I find my hands empty, by having permitted vain glory to rob me of the merit of all my works!

THIRD POINT.—Through this mystery of an Incarnate God we have contracted an alliance with him, by virtue of which we are the brethren of Jesus Christ; nay, the very members of, and even one body with, this God-Man. We are indebted to his humiliation and abjection for this honour and happiness. For, had he not descended from the throne of his glory, but refused to take flesh like ours, he would, indeed, have been our God, and we should have been his creatures; but we never could have enjoyed the advantage of being united to him as brethren, and of becoming his members. Our near alliance, consequently, with him is the fruit of his Humility.

How dearly, then, should I love that abjection, which has elevated me so much in dignity, and has been to me the cause of so much good? And yet I revolt at it, and refuse to embrace it. In my meditations upon it, my heart melts into tears, and I am lost in admiration; or, if I have occasion to treat of it in my sermons, I do it in the most moving terms; but, when an opportunity occurs of practising it, my unction is dried up, and the ardour of my devotion becomes extinguished. The most trifling act of disrespect, or what I merely imagine to be such, is enough to sour my heart against a neighbour; and if I do not resent it, I perhaps dissemble, in order to cherish a more malignant spleen.

Is this paying to God the honour which he deserves, or making him due acknowledgment for the humiliations that he has endured for my sake? In order to raise me to some kind of equality with himself, he did not disdain to assume my infirmities and miseries; yet I have the greatest horror of resembling him in the very point in which he has conferred upon me so singular an honour and advantage. "What a disgrace is it (says St. Bernard) for members to live in ease and delights under a head crowned with thorns!" In like manner, what a perversion is it of reason and right order, to acknowledge myself a member of a Head, who has voluntarily annihilated himself, and yet to be scandalized at his humiliations, and to refuse to take part in them! Is not this equivalent to a total withdrawing of myself from all connexion with him? What else can I expect but that, as a just punishment of my disloyalty, I shall be suffered to languish in sloth, and never to make any progress in virtue? I ought to remember, that *God resists the proud, and gives his grace to the humble* (James iv.); that, to be without Humility is to be void of the christian, and much more of the ecclesiastical, spirit; and that, consequently, without it, no advancement can be made in the ways of God, nor any union subsist between my soul and Him. This is certainly an evil,— a misfortune, which requires an immediate remedy.

Concluding Prayer.—I know, dear Jesus, that pride was the first of all sins, and that from this polluted source has sprung a deluge of crimes, which could not be removed but by Humility. Thy example, then, is a lesson which I well understand. Ah! my Lord, I am confounded when I reflect that thou, the God of heaven, wast enclosed in the womb of a virgin, and didst remain there for nine months hidden and unknown, in order to teach me the duty of becoming humble and little, like a child. I can devise no excuse for not doing as thou hast taught me; for glory cannot be due to me, when thou hast despised it; and the choice made by thee of obscurity convinces me, that I have no title to be known and esteemed.

At present, I feel disposed to suffer the greatest insults, and to be numbered amongst the outcasts of men for thy sake; but these feelings soon pass away, and my good purposes are forgotten, when occasion offers of carrying them into effect. I am sensible that no virtue is more difficult of acquirement, and that none requires greater sacrifices and more violent efforts, than true Humility. Help me, then, O Lord, to overcome my extreme sensibility under injuries; enable me to conquer myself; and strengthen me in the resolution, with which thou now inspirest me, to labour to eradicate from my heart that fund of pride, which is, as it were, engrafted in my nature, and influences the entire conduct of my life.

SECOND MEDITATION.

ON THE POVERTY OF JESUS CHRIST IN HIS BIRTH.

You know the grace of our Lord Jesus Christ, who, when he was rich, for your sakes became poor.—2 COR. viii.

FIRST POINT.—From the very moment of his birth Jesus Christ begins to execute his design of living in Poverty. This divine Majesty, this sovereign Creator of the universe, to whom all things belong, might have been born amidst riches and abundance. This condition even seemed to accord best with the dignity of his person, and the object of his mission. For, coming, as he did, upon earth for the purpose of drawing men to himself and subjecting them to his law, what could be supposed more likely to engage them to follow him, than his assuming the splendour and pomp of earthly greatness? This, at least, was the notion entertained by the Jews of their expected Messias: they believed that he would come in all the magnificence of royalty, and would load his followers with temporal gifts. But, how different are ours from the views of God! This Messias, this Desired of nations, comes at last; but he comes in Poverty: his design being thereby to convince mankind of a truth, which he was afterwards to announce in his gospel, namely, that *the poor are blessed* (Mat. v.).

Example, on an occasion like this, is of more avail than the most eloquent discourse could be. It proves, beyond dispute, the merit and value of poverty, inasmuch as it was the choice of God himself. Nothing can be better calculated to inspire us not only with an esteem, but with a love and relish for that state, than to see it consecrated in the person of our God and Saviour.

Hence, although to embrace a state of actual Poverty by renouncing all worldly possessions, be not commanded, but only recommended, in the gospel, yet, as a Christian, I am strictly and indispensably obliged to be *poor in spirit*, by being at all times in the disposition to give up into the hands of God all that I enjoy—by considering what I have as lent to me during his good pleasure—and by regarding Poverty, when embraced or submitted to from a motive of religion, as *amiable*, by the near alliance which it confers to Jesus Christ—*honourable*, as the state which he chose for himself—and *desirable*, from the special title which it confers to the kingdom of heaven. Nay, when I consider my close affinity to Jesus Christ, my vocation to that ministry in his Church, which he first committed to those only who forsook all things to follow him, and my peculiar obligation of tending to perfection—I cannot doubt but it is my duty to follow the evangelical counsel of Poverty, so far as to lay aside all solicitude and anxiety for the things of this world—to be quite resigned and content under the privations to which I may be subjected—not to implicate myself in secular affairs for the sake of gain—to prove to the world by my general conduct that I have a real and inward contempt for riches—to exercise great charity to the poor in proportion to my means, and to use what I possess with moderation.

SECOND POINT.—If we examine the circumstances attending the birth of our Infant God, we shall find them all to indicate the most abject Poverty, which ever fell to the lot of a human being. In the range of a large city, not a house is to be found where he can be accommodated at his birth with shelter from the inclemency of the weather. After a fruitless search for this purpose by St. Joseph and his virgin spouse, they are compelled to take refuge in a miserable shed erected for cattle. Here our Poor Master is pleased to be born amongst us. The manger is converted into his cradle; his bed is, at best, but a little straw; and his clothing is made of tattered rags. Being now become like unto us, mortal and passible, how sensible must his infant body be of the privations which it endures! How must it feel the rigour of the winter season, and the want of something more than it has to defend it from the night cold! But no extremity of Poverty and wretchedness can be imagined, to which he is not willing to submit for our sakes.

Oh! what impressive lessons may be drawn from this stable, this straw, and these rags of our Infant Jesus! Were I not otherwise assured to the contrary, could I contemplate my Master in the stable of Bethelem without believing his state of Poverty and misery to be an implicit command to every one of his disciples to renounce all worldly possessions, as did the primitive Christians? But, whilst I know that this degree of Poverty is not required of me, can I be deaf to the condemnation here pronounced by Jesus Christ against that spirit of avarice, which pervades the world, and from which even his ministers are far from being exempt? What I here behold should teach me the necessity of keeping my soul undefiled by the least taint of this odious vice. It should convince me that no good qualities can possibly redeem so foul a stain in one obliged by his vocation to inculcate to others disinterestedness and Poverty of spirit—that, if I pass for a priest who is fond of money, this total want of resemblance to my Master will justly render me despicable to all: and that, by thus losing the esteem and confidence of those entrusted to my charge, my ministry will be in a great degree fruitless.

Convinced, as I must be, of the necessity of my being *poor in spirit*, I cannot be too careful in scrutinizing the dispositions of my heart and my general conduct with reference to money and temporal prosperity. Stooping my head this day to go under the humble shed of Bethlehem, and there taking my station beside Jesus in the manger, I should endeavour to conceive a contempt for riches, by meditating on the vanity and instability of the goods of this world, and animating myself to confidence in that kind Providence, who never abandons the care of his faithful servants.—If I study the doctrine of those great and holy men, who in their Poverty have been faithful imitators of my Master, I shall see cause to dread the illusions of the demon of avarice, who often tries to insinuate his poison into the heart of a poor Pastor, by suggesting the idea of the great good which more ample means would enable him to effect: it will teach me that, where self-interest is concerned, excuses are seldom wanting for abandoning the finest projects in favour of religion and charity—that money is of itself a temptation, and that, if God give it to me, without a powerful grace to use it well, I may, and probably shall, abuse it. In short, the maxims of the saints will teach me that, under all privations, I ought not to murmur, but console myself by meditating on the declaration of the Apostle, that *they, who will become rich, fall into temptation and into the snare of the devil, and into many unprofitable and hurtful desires, which drown men in destruction and perdition: for covetousness is the root of all evils; which some desiring have erred from the faith, and have entangled themselves in many sorrows* (1 Tim. vi.).

THIRD POINT.—Another duty, to which the Poverty, that I behold in the stable of Bethlehem, cannot fail to draw my attention, is the great Gospel precept of charity to the poor. I cannot contemplate the privations of Jesus, without feelings of compassion and sympathy, and a desire to render him all possible relief and comfort. This he has assured me I may do, by exercising charity to his poor members. Nothing but a lively faith can be wanting to make me behold Jesus Christ in every object of distress that meets my eye. So essential in a true Christian is liberality to the poor, that it may be termed the touchstone of solid virtue. No virtue is more necessary or more amiable in a Pastor. On himself it draws down numberless blessings; and to the poor it is a source of abundant relief, for the rich are oftentimes induced by his example to give what they would otherwise withhold, and they readily make him the distributer of their charities. Then, how sweet it is to dry up the tear of the widow, and to become a father to the helpless orphan! He, who rewarded the liberality of Abraham by sending him angels for his guests—who rescued Lot from the flames of Sodom on account of his charity—who recompensed the widow that harboured Elias, by multiplying her oil—and who raised to life the son of the Sunamite woman, for receiving the prophet Eliseus—will not be unmindful of the good Pastor, who feeds the hungry, gives drink to the thirsty, and clothes the naked.

It is of importance that I should here examine, what use I make of the ecclesiastical property which comes into my hands. If what I receive from that source be more than sufficient for my decent maintenance, I cannot doubt, but that I am strictly bound to apply the superfluity either to the relief of the distressed, or to some other charitable or religious purpose; and, in so doing, I ought not to suppose that I have so much the merit of charity as of performing my duty. So generally is the doctrine of St. Bernard on this subject received in the Church, that it would be the greatest rashness not to adhere to it in practice. "Whatever (says that enlightened Father) you receive from the altar, beyond what is necessary for food and clothing, is not your own; and in keeping it, you are guilty of sacrilege." And again: "The naked and the hungry cry out and complain, that what you uselessly squander away is theirs, and is cruelly withheld from them." I know this to be the universal doctrine of the Fathers of the Church; and what once was true in this respect is true still.

CONCLUDING PRAYER.—O God, the Creator of heaven and earth, but whom I here adore under the form of a helpless Infant in a manger! I am sensible, that the state of Poverty which it was thy pleasure to embrace, and from which thou didst never depart, was designed to teach me, that all earthly goods are empty and vain; and that, to be rich for eternity, it is necessary that I should be *poor in spirit*. Unwilling to forego the joys of thy kingdom and the never-failing riches of thy glory, for all that the world can either give or take away, behold, I now cheerfully commit to thy care, and place at thy disposal, whatever I possess. Henceforth I will only consider myself as the steward of what thou permittest to come into my hands. Grant me the grace not to place my affections upon what thou didst despise; so that, should it please thee, as perhaps it may, to take from me either all or any part of my possessions, I may be disposed to say, with all the resignation and disinterestedness of holy Job: *the Lord hath given, and the Lord hath taken away; blessed be his name* (Job. i.). Nay more; if thou, who knowest the secrets of my heart better than I do, seest therein any lurking attachment to what I enjoy, which is displeasing to thee, rather take it from me altogether, than leave it in my hands with the danger of its drowning me in destruction.

Why, my dear Master, should I not be content to be like thee? Or, why should I fix any part of my affections on what thou didst ever try, both by word and example, to make me despise? When I contemplate the wretched fate of the apostate Judas and look at my own frailty, I cannot but fear to indulge the least particle of avarice, which I know would soon increase, and in time might lead me also to betray thee. Save me, then,

O Lord, through thy mercy, in the way thou knowest best; and never let it be my misfortune, as it has been that of thousands, to bring discredit upon the sacred ministry by the cursed love of money. Let it rather be my constant study, to keep my heart pure from the infection of avarice, by exercising a boundless liberality towards thy poor members, purely for thy honour and for the love of thee. Above all, forbid, O Jesus, that I should ever hoard up, or unlawfully squander away, the sacred deposit placed in my hands for the purposes of religion and charity. It is, at present, my sincere resolution not to do it; do thou always enable me by thy grace to fulfil my purpose.

THIRD MEDITATION.

ON THE OBEDIENCE OF JESUS CHRIST IN HIS FLIGHT INTO EGYPT.

He humbled himself, becoming obedient.—PHIL. ii.

FIRST POINT.—Although the divine order, which was communicated by the ministry of an angel to Joseph, to flee into Egypt with Jesus and Mary, was not addressed immediately to Jesus Christ himself, yet it regarded him; and, from the full knowledge which this

Infant-God had of all that was passing, his immediate and hasty flight may be justly considered as an act of Obedience on his part to the will of his heavenly Father.

This Obedience was most holy in its motive, being grounded upon a perfect conformity of his will to the will of his Father, whom alone he sought to please, and in whom alone he placed his confidence. Him he beheld, not only in the heavenly messenger, but also in Joseph, who, on this occasion, was to act the part of a minister of God. This divine Infant, therefore, suffered himself to be carried off, without any other thought but of filial submission and entire resignation of his interests into the hands of Providence. The whole of our divine Master's conduct, on this occasion, is an excellent model of the Obedience which the subordinate Pastors of the Church owe to their Superiors. The foundation of this Obedience is holy, for it contains a most heroic act of faith, an excellent act of hope and confidence, and a perfect act of charity.

1st, It contains a most heroic act of *faith*, because by Obedience I profess my belief, that a divine authority is vested in the bishop, to whose jurisdiction I am subject, and that he is really appointed by the Holy Ghost to rule his portion of the Church of God—a truth of which I am as certain as if I were assured of it by the living voice of Jesus

Christ. Hence it is my duty at all times to shew that Obedience to my spiritual Superior, which is due to divine authority, and to consider him as holding the place of God in my regard. This Obedience to my bishop I solemnly promised at my ordination to the priesthood; and since his jurisdiction holds good independently of any frailty or imperfection to which he may be subject, it follows that I ought, on all occasions, to respect his authority, and to consider his lawful commands as the commands of God himself.

2d, By this Obedience I exercise a most excellent act of *hope* and confidence. Taking the light of reason for my sole guide, I might sometimes have cause to fear, that implicit Obedience might lead me astray. But, knowing the authority of him, whom I obey, to be divine, if I submit my own judgment to his, I have the firmest grounds to hope that God, in reward of my Obedience, will inspire him to direct me in the way most pleasing to himself—that he will not suffer the situation, to which I am appointed, to be an occasion of my spiritual ruin—that he will deliver me from the dangers to which I am therein exposed—and, in short, that he will be well pleased with, and will reward, what I do in a true spirit of dependence.

3d, I herein make, also, a perfect act of divine *charity*, because the greatest sacrifice, which I can offer to the Deity, is that of my own will, and nothing but a pure love of God can induce me to renounce what I esteem above all the gifts of nature. What a source of consolation is here for an obedient ecclesiastic! But when, on the contrary, I murmur, am dissatisfied, and seek means of evading the orders of my bishop, what just cause have I not to fear, that I am offending God? *It is not you* (said the Almighty to Samuel, speaking of the Jews when they had demanded a king for their ruler), *it is not you they have rejected, but me* (1 Kings viii.). When I, in like manner, fail in Obedience, it is God himself whom I disobey: I set myself up against him, and both in will and in deed reject his authority.

Second Point.—The Obedience of Jesus Christ was not less difficult of execution than it was holy in its motive. In his delicate state of infancy he had to leave his own country—to be exposed to the fatigues and dangers of a long journey into a foreign land—to set out, without delay, preparation or provision, on the very night on which the order was given—to go and take up his abode among a race of people, strangers to the true God and enemies to the Jewish name—to live there in obscurity, poverty, and want—and there to remain until recalled by the will and command of Providence.

Notwithstanding all these difficulties, no

demur was made, but Joseph *arose and took the child and his mother by night, and retired into Egypt* (Matt. ii.). To regard this command with human eyes (as is too often done under similar circumstances) a thousand reasons might have been found to excuse Obedience. How was a new-born infant to endure the hardships of such a journey? Would not many hazards have to be encountered on the way? How was provision to be made for their subsistence, when at their journey's end? Could no more practicable plan be devised of escaping the persecution of Herod?—Is not my reasoning similar to this, when the duties imposed upon me are at variance with my humour and inclination? Have I not a repugnance to use due exertion to overcome the obstacles opposed to the execution of my duty? Am I not troubled in mind and offended, if my Superior yields not to my representations and remonstrances? And do I not attribute his firmness, however prudent in itself, to an overruling and unfeeling rigour? Such conduct is not conformable to the example set me by Jesus Christ, and to that spirit of ready and cheerful Obedience which he requires me to pay to the rulers of his Church. It is a sign that I am a stranger to the value of that subordination which is necessary to preserve peace, unanimity, and concord, in the fold of Christ. It proves that I am not aware that, in the kingdom of Jesus, those are the greatest and the most pleasing in his sight, who are the most obedient and submissive. It shews, in short, that I have neither the faith, nor the hope, nor the charity of one, who is seriously convinced that the Holy Ghost is the author of the dependence which has been established in the church of God.

There is not a more certain mark of a Priest's being under the guidance of the Spirit of God than when he shews a ready and cheerful disposition to holy Obedience. On the other hand, from the contempt of this divine ordinance suggested by human pride, almost all the heresies and schisms, which have troubled the Church and withdrawn millions from the one fold of the one shepherd, have taken their rise. Hence I ought to dread the least guilt of disobedience, and to consider as addressed to me, as much as to the rest of the faithful, these words of the Apostle: *let every soul be subject to the higher powers . . . for those who resist acquire damnation to themselves. Be subject, therefore, from necessity, not only on account of anger, but for conscience sake* (Rom. xiii.). I ought to regard my bishop as the ordinary and natural judge of whatever concerns religion, as having a right to decide on all questions of faith and morality, to regulate the ecclesiastical government of his diocese or district, and to make such statutes and ordinances as he may judge to be expedient, provided they be not at variance with the general discipline and canons of the Church. Such being the order of Church government founded by Jesus Christ, I cannot form too high an idea of, or be too exact in paying Obedience to, this divine authority.

THIRD POINT.—The obedience of Jesus Christ in his flight to Egypt was rewarded by the consequences which it produced.— 1st, Our divine Saviour carried with him into that country those salutary graces, which sanctified it, and made its desert plains worthy to become, in after times, the abode of thousands of holy solitaries and penitents, whose angelic lives were the edification and admiration of the Christian world. And 2d, It saved him from the violence of the impious persecutor who sought his life, and delivered him from sharing in the horrible massacre to which so many Innocents fell victims.

Were I fully sensible of the fruits and advantages of Obedience, I should, under all occurrences, cheerfully embrace it, and should even dread to undertake any change without the free choice and unbiassed call of my bishop; and, on the other hand, with these I should be content in any situation, however mean or however laborious. Whatever charge I undertake, Obedience will ennoble it in my eyes, and will make it more sweet and agreeable than any other can possibly be. Obedience will draw down upon my labours special blessings and graces from the Almighty. When, and *only when*, I act by the ordinance of God, what I do is properly his work; and *then only* is he pledged to support me, and to crown my endeavours with success. If I were well convinced of this great truth, I should be content with the portion of our Lord's vineyard assigned to my care: to it I should carefully and zealously devote the labours of my life, and studiously guard against the suggestions of corrupt nature, should it tempt me to seek greater ease, emolument, or honour in another place. Even if I am certain that my talents are equal to a more important situation than I at present fill, the increased danger and responsibility attending such a situation should induce me to leave it to my Superior to find out my abilities, and await in silence his command. In a word, a true spirit of Obedience will teach me to regard the very place where I am fixed, or to which my bishop may wish to appoint me, as the one destined for me by God, and in which I am the most likely to be successful in the edification and sanctification of my neighbour, and my own advancement in virtue and interior happiness.

Another advantage of Obedience is, to preserve me from the assaults of the most dangerous and tyrannical enemy that I have to fear in the road to perfection and salvation, my own self-will. By Obedience this is kept under restraint and in subjection to the will of God. Under the guidance and direction of the divine will, which is ever right and holy, I am always secure. As long as I walk in the way which God has marked out for me through the voice of his vicegerent, I must be doing what is most pleasing to him, and there can be no danger of my going astray. Hence there is no more solid virtue, nor more transcendent merit, than what is founded on Obedience. Without it the most splendid virtue is so but in appearance, and what the world regards as meritorious actions are but the workings of self-love.

Is my conduct regulated by these maxims? Perhaps my Superior has disposed of me in a manner suited to my views and wishes. —If so, I do not complain.—But, if my situation possess no other advantages but those of enabling me to advance in the humble path of perfection, and to acquire glory and merit only in the sight of God, or if it in any way require a sacrifice of my own will and inclination, do I not, by yielding to discontent, shew that I am insensible to these advantages? Such conduct not only renders me unworthy of the happiness of which I am in quest, but is often a source of real misery, and the occasion of numberless sins.

CONCLUDING PRAYER.—My God, I firmly believe that, in order to my success in the holy ministry, thou shouldst direct me to the situation wherein thou wouldst have me to labour. This direction I cannot hope to obtain otherwise than through the voice of my Superior, in hearing and obeying whom thou hast assured me that I hear and obey thyself. Confirm me, then, O Lord, in the path of Obedience. For this end, give me a true simplicity of mind and docility of heart. With the former I shall refrain from reasoning on what I am commanded to do, leaving thee to examine the motives of him whom thou hast placed over me; and with the latter I shall seldom have objections or remonstrances to oppose to his commands. Should I even be at a loss to justify his orders in my own interior, still I shall obey. This, I am convinced, is the safest road to true happiness and content of mind. For, how can I fail to enjoy these, or what can ever rob me of them, when I know that by Obedience I am doing thy will and honouring thee, promoting the sanctification of my neighbour, and working out my own salvation? These, my God, are the sole objects of my ambition; and oh! I pray that I may never, through obstinacy and disobedience, deviate from the sure and beaten path, which conducts to thee.

CONSIDERATION.

ON CONVERSATION WITH OUR NEIGHBOUR.

It is the duty of every priest, and much more of priests who have the care of souls, to be guarded and circumspect in Conversation, that they may avoid the many faults and abuses which insinuate themselves into discourse in general. The eyes of the world are in a particular manner upon us, and on no occasion, so much as in Conversation, are we apt to betray our weaknesses and imperfections. So true is this, that we are assured by the Spirit of God that *he who offends not in words, the same is a perfect man* (James iii.). That our Conversation may be as perfect as is consistent with human frailty, we must observe the following rules :—1st, To let it ever be accompanied by modesty and reserve ;—2d, To let it be solid and useful ; —and 3d, To let it on all occasions be influenced by charity and a desire to promote harmony and peace.

First Point.—Our Conversation must be accompanied by modesty and reserve. The world has certain laws of propriety and decorum to regulate its own Conversation, but to us are assigned others more severe and rigid, which we are always expected to observe: for many things may be said by a man of the world, that would not be regarded as offensive to propriety, or are, at least, sanctioned by usage, which would sound very ill and be very reprehensible from the mouth of a priest. To us, therefore, we may consider as particularly addressed, that injunction of the apostle: *let your modesty be known unto all men* (Phil. iv.). This modesty must appear in the air of our countenance, in our general deportment, in our gestures, in the tone of our voice, and in the terms and expressions which we make use of. Without herein aiming at what is unnatural or has the appearance of study and affectation, we may and ought to avoid certain fantastical and ridiculous airs, too much gesticulation, a too elevated and pompous tone of voice, and numberless familiar words and expressions, which, however innocent in themselves, accord not with the received notions respecting clerical decorum.

It is an error to suppose that, by habitually indulging in merry and unreserved Conversation, a priest makes himself agreeable, and gains esteem and confidence. On the contrary, the world is the most discerning and severe censor that we have to dread. It knows the bounds which we ought to observe, and what we owe to the sanctity of our profession; and, however licentious and disorderly it may be itself, it expects from us the most scrupulous propriety in Conversation. In the discourse of a priest, it looks for a certain degree of thoughtfulness, gravity, moderation, and wisdom; and, where it meets with such a character, that man is a subject of edification to it and the object of its confidence. The opposite character, at best, serves only for its amusement.

It is a received maxim, that the mouth speaks from the abundance of the heart.—When a priest, therefore, is observed to display the worldling in his manner of Conversation, it is invariably attributed to interior dissipation. A person habituated to recollection and a sense of the divine presence, as a priest should be, necessarily feels restrained from giving full scope to the vivacity of nature. He is open and affable; yet in moderation. He is neither morose nor melancholy; yet in his demonstrations of joy, he never entirely loses sight of gravity. He observes not a sullen silence; but neither does he try to engross the whole Conversation. He speaks his sentiments with candour and simplicity; but he allows to others the opportunity of doing the same, and is at least as willing to listen as to speak. How many faults should we avoid in Conversation, and how much more respect should we procure for our sacred character, were we always to keep these rules in view?

Second Point.—Our Conversation must be solid and useful. By this we are not to understand, that it should necessarily, or even generally, turn upon spiritual subjects. Still it is greatly to be deplored, that, in the intercourse which the ministers of God keep up with the laity, allusion should so seldom be made to the *one thing necessary*—the great affair of salvation. Many priests might be supposed to be forbidden the exercise of their divine commission everywhere save within the walls of the house of God, so silent are they on all other occasions on matters relating to piety. It is true, that such allusions may occasionally be ill-timed, and that, consequently, they must be introduced with prudence. It must, also, be admitted that Conversation is not to be converted into a sermon. But, after all, two things are certain:—1st, That men in general are not so liable, as some may imagine, to be disgusted by a sentiment of piety now and then introduced by a priest into Conversation; and that what would be turned into ridicule, if it proceeded from the lips of a worldling, will generally meet with attention and respect when it comes from him:—And 2d, That to give expression to a well-timed sentiment of religion, is often more impressive than a formal discourse, and is followed by the happiest consequences; whilst, on the other hand, it is frequently a matter of surprise with the laity that priests so seldom remind them of their obligations to their great Master, their neighbours, and themselves.

On his own account, too, it must be admitted that the general tenor of a priest's Conversation should be on solid and useful subjects. For if, after having spent some time in company, which has filled his mind with a crowd of vain and frivolous ideas, he retires, and (as generally happens) has to place himself again in the presence of God, how can he pray with relish, unction, or attention? It is a truth, to which many can bear testimony from their own experience, that from the generality of worldly company a priest can carry home nothing but an empty heart, a disordered imagination, and a great dryness and disrelish for the things of God.

THIRD POINT.—Our Conversation must be charitable and inoffensive. It is but too true, that we can rarely retire from company, and examine all that is past, without finding some cause to fear that we have violated the precept of fraternal charity. This may happen in many ways; but the most frequent are the following:—1st, From a natural impatience and sourness of mind many are apt to contract a habit of speaking in an angry and forbidding manner: no matter what precaution may be taken, to speak to them is to lay one's self open to a repulsive answer.—2nd, There are two characters that can hardly go into company without falling into contentions and disputes destructive of, or prejudicial to, charity. The one is prone to contradiction; the other is obstinate. The former, through a mere spirit of contradiction, will find some objection to every sentiment or argument that is advanced; the latter, through obstinacy, will never yield or own himself in the wrong.—3d, Many are apt to indulge too much in raillery and ridicule; and others show an extreme sensibility, by taking offence when none is intended.—With difficulty are the former ever restrained from gratifying their unfeeling propensity, and seldom do they stop to think, whether what they are about to say is calculated to give pain or not. The offence taken may, indeed, oftentimes be the effect of too great sensibility on the part of the person offended; yet not only Christian charity, but the received rules of propriety, require that we should be always upon our guard, so as not to wound the feelings of a neighbour.—4th, Nothing is more common in Conversation, than rashly to judge the motives of other people, and to take a malignant satisfaction in condemning the conduct of the absent.—

CONSIDERATION. 165

But, lastly, the great bane of Conversation, and the cause of numberless sins, is the detestable and mean vice of detraction; and, however little occasion we may have to be particularly cautioned against the faults already noticed, it is certain, and greatly to be lamented, that many persons, in other respects remarkable for great delicacy and timidity of conscience, are, with reference to detraction, far from being as timid as they ought to be.

It is the province of charity to banish all these defects from Conversation. Far from every Christian, and farther still from every priest, should be the outward expression of passion or impatience. If he cannot at all times restrain the interior motions of his heart, he should, at least, keep his tongue under due control.—Contradictions and disputes should be studiously avoided. From the moment that a question at issue begins to assume the air of a quarrel, it is better to be silent than obstinately to aim at an empty triumph over an adversary to the detriment of charity and mutual good feeling.—On the subject of ridicule and raillery it may be observed, that, although a little humour at the expense of a third person, who takes it in good part, be not censurable, yet the habit of indulging in it is far from being a pleasing trait in the character of a priest. But when there is danger of giving offence (as there often is) it would ill become him to turn his neighbour into ridicule, and to seek amusement at the expense of the feelings of another party. — With reference to Conversation grounded on rash judgment, or a malignant feeling towards the absent, to name it is sufficient to create a due horror of it.—But as for detraction, it cannot be held in too great abhorrence, nor is it possible for any person to have on this head too timorous and tender a conscience. Let it, therefore, be our indispensable rule, to speak well of all persons, or, if there be any of whom we can say nothing good, to be silent.

Sixth Day.

FIRST MEDITATION.

ON THE HIDDEN LIFE OF JESUS CHRIST.

He went down with them to Nazareth, and was subject to them.—LUKE ii.

FIRST POINT.—The Retirement of our divine Master from his infancy until the period when he entered upon his public mission, is a mystery not less deserving of our admiration than those which appear more brilliant. Filled as he was with all the treasures of wisdom and knowledge—possessed in a super-eminent degree of all the gifts of nature and of grace—having had it in his power to work numberless miracles for the glory of his Father, to convert sinners and idolaters, and to diffuse his Church over the whole earth—and having even come down from heaven for these very purposes—still this Man-God embraced a hidden and retired life; and of the three-and-thirty years, which he spent upon earth, he passed thirty in Retirement and obscurity, reserving only three for his public ministry, and the announcement of the Kingdom of God.

What was the occupation of our heavenly Master during all these years? He was obedient to Mary and Joseph. This is all we know upon the subject:—the rest is buried in obscurity, and known only to God. Surprising as this may at first sight appear, it is not difficult to determine the motive of our Master's conduct. He came to be a model to mankind, and especially to those whom he destined for the work of the ministry. And what a lesson does he here give us in condemnation of that desire of external show, which is the source of so many disorders, or, at least, prevents so many of us from ever attaining the true perfection of our state? A Pastor of souls cannot possibly arrive at solid virtue, or be a fit instrument in the hands of God for the guidance of souls, unless he be an interior man; and what more powerful inducement can he have to aim at that perfection, than to know that his Master spent thirty years of his life in Retirement totally unknown to the world?

In vain, after this, will artful self-love endeavour to persuade me, that an interior life is incompatible with zeal for the glory of God and the salvation of souls,—that it is at variance with the duties which I owe to Society, and repugnant to true charity,—and that great Retirement would render me and my talents in a great measure useless. The example of Jesus Christ proves all this to be at best, mere specious reasoning. Am I better qualified than he was, to advance the glory of God? Or can I be more interested than he in the welfare and salvation of my neighbour? Do I know better than he did, how to fulfil the duties of social life? Or, is greater fruit to be expected from my talents than from his? Ah! vain soul, learn to undeceive thyself, and be confounded at thy presumption. Instead of the maxims of a disguised worldly spirit, my Saviour is come to instil into me very different principles; he is come to teach me to love to be unknown, forsaken, and forgotten—to attend quietly to the discharge of the functions of my ministry—and not to implicate myself in the distracting embarrassments and intrigues of secular affairs.

SECOND POINT.—Although we know not what were the particular occupations of Jesus Christ during his retired life, yet it is not to be doubted but that they were of the lowest and most ordinary kind. We may suppose, that he passed many of his hours in manual labour with his reputed father, that he shared with his mother in the care of their little family affairs, and executed with dutiful punctuality the various offices which they prescribed to him. What an occupation for the great Messias, the envoy of heaven, and the only son of God! Yet the Almighty derived as much glory from these actions as from the splendid works which this Saviour of mankind afterwards performed. What made them so meritorious and agreeable in the eyes of his Father was their being all done in strict conformity with his will, being animated by an interior Spirit, and enhanced by purely divine motives.

There were at that time many renowned and powerful princes upon the earth. Conquerors were making the world resound with the glory of their names, and the fame of their actions. Their designs, enterprises, and exploits were the general theme of admiration, and were everywhere published and proclaimed. But, in the estimation of the Deity all these performances were nothing, because they were not referred to him. On the other hand, Jesus Christ was not spoken of: his name, his birth, his abode and occupation were all equally unknown to the world. He was dwelling in a corner of Judea, in as much obscurity as if he were not in existence. But the eyes of his Father were fixed upon him as an object of his dearest complacency, and all his actions were of infinite value in the sight of heaven.

What a source of instruction as well as of consolation are these reflections for a poor and humble Pastor or missionary, who, being placed in an obscure situation, has no opportunity of attracting the notice of the world! What an encouragement to him to persevere in the zealous and faithful discharge of his lowly duties! Truly may it be said of him, that *he is dead, and his life is hidden with Christ in God* (Col. iii.) : and that, for this very reason his life is most agreeable to the Almighty, and most conformable to the Spirit and sentiments of Jesus Christ. What more can a sincere Christian and a true Pastor of souls desire, than to be thus intimately united to God, and to enjoy the honour of so near an affinity and resemblance to his Master and model? In this union with God and this affinity to Jesus Christ consists the essence of an interior life; and in such a life there is nothing, however despicable in appearance, which is not deserving of the highest esteem. It would be a decided violation of the first and most essential principles of religion, to regulate our esteem of things by any other standard than that of the sanctity and perfection, which they derive from being done in conformity with the will of God. This renders the meanest action that can be performed of inestimable value.

THIRD POINT.—Great were the peace and tranquillity of soul enjoyed by Jesus Christ during the years of his Retirement. Unknown to the world, he was neither exposed to its censure, nor liable to its contradictions.

Confined within the narrow precincts of a poor habitation and engaged in manual labour, he had no share in the turmoils which agitated the rest of men. He quietly enjoyed the silence and calm of solitude ; and his sole entertainment was with his heavenly Father, from whom he received without interruption the sweetest consolations.

Of all earthly blessings, peace of mind is doubtless one of the most precious and desirable ; and it is not less certain, that the surest means to attain it is to lead a quiet and retired life. The world is like a tempestuous sea : Retirement is a port to shelter us from the storm. Herein consists the happiness of a religious life—a happiness so obvious even to the votaries of the world, that, by their own acknowledgment, the religious in his cell is a thousand times more content than they are amidst the enjoyments, whereby they try to counterbalance the troubles and embarrassments inseparable from common life.

Broad as is the line of separation between the two states in many respects, still to imitate, as nearly as is consistent with his duty, the happy retirement of the recluse should be the desire and aim of every Pastor. He, who is truly alive to the spirit and end of his vocation, will faithfully and rigorously discharge every external duty ; but, the less these duties are attended with outward show, the more agreeable they will be to him. And, having done his duty, he will be happy to think that he has nothing more to do with the world — that the world has no further claim upon him—and that he can pass by unregarded these thousands of events, which are the source of endless pain and vexation to worldlings. He will be indifferent to every occurrence, in which neither duty nor charity demand his interference.

But alas! how many priests forfeit their happiness for want of cultivating a spirit of Retirement. In solitude they are a burden to themselves, and, consequently, they are never by choice alone. Rather than not be doing something, they go abroad and meddle with affairs which in no way concern them, and in which they are sure to meet with something to disturb their peace of mind. Although they thus find by experience, that it is impossible to enter into the affairs of the world without meeting with much to excite passions quite inconsistent with interior tranquillity, still Retirement grows more and more irksome to them; so that, whether they be at home or abroad, they are a prey to vexation and disgust. Oh! why will we not, even for the sake of our present happiness, seek from God and from ourselves in holy retirement what we shall look for in vain elsewhere?

CONCLUDING PRAYER.—Blessed for ever, O my God, be thy infinite mercy and goodness, for having taught me, by thy own example, the secure road to present and future happiness. I am sincerely determined, as far as the duties of my state will allow me, to lead a hidden and retired life, and to be upon my guard against all the secret suggestions, whereby self-love seeks to draw me into the embarrassments of worldly affairs. I will daily study the heavenly maxims, which thy retired life unfolds to me, and which I clearly discover to be the only sure guides to lasting peace. Give me a relish—a daily increasing love—for a life of holy retirement. Disengage my heart from all the vain amusements and perplexing cares of the world, which have hitherto distracted my mind, and kept me from an union with thee. Inspire me with a true interior spirit, so that, should every other source of consolation fail me, I may find an abundance of peace in my own breast.

I desire nothing but thee, my God; and, whilst I should seek thee in vain amid the noise and tumult of the world, I know thou art to be found in the most dreary solitude. Lead me, then into retirement, and I will there entertain myself with thee; there I will speak to thee; there I will listen to thy voice, and relish thy hidden sweetness. What am I, O Lord, without thee? and possessing thee, what more can I desire? What does it matter to me, whether I am courted or despised by the world, provided I have thee for an approving witness of my actions, and enjoy the honour of thy consoling presence in my own interior? Henceforth thou shalt be to me in lieu of every other comfort. I will shut myself out so entirely from the cares and distractions of the world, that I may be able to address thee without ceasing in the language of one of thy most devoted servants—" My Lord and my All."

SECOND MEDITATION.

ON THE CHARITY OF JESUS CHRIST IN HIS ACTIVE LIFE.

This is my commandment, that you love one another as I have loved you.—JOHN xv.

FIRST POINT.—When Jesus Christ had attained the age of thirty years, he began to manifest himself to the world for the purpose of preaching his gospel. Having now to treat with all sorts of persons, he found an extensive field open before him for the exercise of Charity—a virtue particularly necessary for all those who, like him, are employed in the work of converting sinners and saving souls. The Charity of our divine Master during his public life was mild, beneficent, and universal. My Charity must resemble his, otherwise it will not be genuine.

In the first place, the Charity of Jesus Christ was *mild*. His inward meekness and humility of heart displayed itself on all occasions, and in every possible way; so that mildness was one of the most remarkable traits in his character. It appeared in his exterior deportment, in his invariable reserve and modesty on all occasions—in his patient endurance of the defects of a grossly ignorant and carnal people—and in his kindness to those incredulous creatures to whom he announced his heavenly truths. With what condescension did he not accommodate himself to their stubborn dispositions, in order to persuade them to believe his doctrine, and to gain them to God? Did he ever resent the trying opposition and insults that he met with from his enemies? What pains did he not take to form his apostles, who were men without name, education, or intelligence? Frequently, when engaged in instructing them, he was obliged to repeat and explain his lessons over and over again. Often was he compelled to interpose his authority, in order to silence their bickerings and disputes; and yet, notwithstanding the disgust which he must have felt on witnessing their imperfections, he lived constantly amongst them ; and, so far from wishing to keep them at a distance, he would never allow them to be absent from him. By this mildness in his general deportment did Jesus Christ acquire a right to say to his apostles and to all future ministers of his gospel, *learn of me, because I am meek and humble of heart* (Matt. xi.). Have I as yet learnt this lesson of meekness ? Have I learnt to bear in a spirit of Charity, with the weaknesses, the defects, the rudeness, and the ignorance of those amongst whom I am employed ?

Nothing is more certain than that ignorance is the source of innumerable evils and disorders in the fold of Christ—that thousands are running headlong to eternal perdition, for want of knowing the great truths which faith teaches, and the duties which it imposes, or because their knowledge is so superficial and imperfect, as to leave their minds unenlightened and their hearts unmoved. From this it follows that one of the first duties of a Pastor is to be assiduous in catechising, instructing, and preaching—offices which require not only much mental and bodily exertion, but also great patience and forbearance. If I fail to imitate the Charity of the Son of God in this part of my ministry, many souls will unquestionably perish, who would otherwise be placed in the way of salvation. As their friend, I should treat them with affability and kindness—as their father, I should seek to gain their confidence and affection—and, as one sent to propagate the kingdom of God, I should make myself *all to all, that I may gain all* (1 Cor. ix.). Woe, then, to me if I discourage, intimidate, and disgust them by any severe and uncharitable language, or by a cold and distant behaviour. On the other hand, I know that my Master has pronounced a blessing on the meek: *blessed are the meek, for they shall possess the land* (Mat. v.). Am I of the number of the meek? or does not my conscience reproach me with having failed, on many occasions, to show a charitable indulgence towards the weakness and ignorance of those with whom I have had to treat? Have I not manifested impatience with children in particular, by severe and angry words, which I was quite sensible were misplaced, and more calculated to do harm than good? This is not copying the Charity of Jesus Christ.

SECOND POINT.—The love which prompted our Saviour to bear with mildness and patience the imperfections of men, and never to intermit his labours in preaching and instructing, induced him likewise to exert his divine power in loading them with benefits. His charity was truly *beneficent. He went about doing good and healing all that were oppressed by the devil* (Acts x.): consoling the afflicted, curing the sick, raising the dead to life, announcing the kingdom of God, and labouring without intermission for the salvation of souls.

Oh! what lessons are here for me and every Pastor of souls! Happy are we if we practise them:—unhappy, if in them we only read our condemnation. To us, indeed, it is not given to work miracles in favour of men: we cannot restore sight to the blind, hearing to the deaf, speech to the dumb, strength to the infirm, and life to the dead. But (to say nothing of the corporal works of mercy, which we are able to perform,—which Jesus Christ encourages us to practise by the assurance that he will regard as done to himself, what we do to his poor and suffering members,—and which ever form a prominent feature in the character of a good shepherd) are there not charitable offices of a spiritual kind to be performed in favour of the souls of men, of which the beneficent miracles of our heavenly Master were emblematical? If we cannot give sight to those who are born blind, and speech to such as are dumb by nature, we can impart knowledge to little ones, and teach them to lisp the praises of God:—if we cannot cure the leprosy, we can cleanse souls which are infected with the spiritual leprosy of sin:—

if we cannot promise him, whose servant lies sick, that we will come and heal him, we can be diligent in attending and administering the sacraments to the infirm:—if we cannot gladden the heart of the widow by restoring her dead son to life, we can unfold to those in affliction the divine consolations of religion:—if we cannot call another Lazarus from the grave, we can embrace numberless opportunities of raising unhappy sinners from the death of sin to the life of grace. These works, which are miracles in the order of grace, and consequently of a more noble kind than such as merely benefit the body, we are enabled to perform: we have solemnly devoted our lives to the performance of them; and it is by performing them, not with an air of coldness, indifference, and disrelish, but with all the solicitude, kindness and attention of an affectionate father, that we are to imitate our beneficent Master, who went about doing good to all. —We must here carefully examine, what resemblance our Charity bears to that of Jesus Christ. And, on this important subject, a general review of the past will not suffice; we must descend to particulars; for, to let one soul perish through the omission of any part of our duty, is to involve ourselves in the same sad and almost irretrievable ruin.

THIRD POINT.—The Charity of Jesus Christ was admirable also from its extent; for it was *universal*. Being sent by his Father for the benefit of all men, and loving all for his Father's sake, he divided his attention and care amongst all, without exception of persons. Never was he known to manifest disgust at the miseries of the poor, or to be influenced by partiality towards the great and rich. Even to those, from whom he received nothing but injustice and opposition, he was disposed to do all possible good; and the graces, of which he was the dispenser, were open to them on their having proper recourse to him. Nay, he called, he invited and pressed them to come to him; and, however hardened and rebellious they might be, whilst he threatened them with his vengeance, he was careful to make them offers of his mercy.

If my Charity be not universal, it is false; for the divine motive, on which true Charity is founded, excludes the possibility of any exception. To extend it, therefore, to some, and to withhold it from others, is altogether to destroy it. Can I charge myself with no partiality destructive of real Charity? Do I not shew a studied kindness to some, whilst I behave with harshness and severity to others? Or, at least, are my language and conduct towards individuals varied only by motives of prudence, and by a conviction that, under existing circumstances, what I say or do is for the best? Do I not prove myself to be an exceptor of persons, and give cause for suspicion that I am rather a seeker of my own temporal interest, than of the general good of all, by behaving with harshness to the hardened sinner, who happens to be poor and mean, whilst I pay marked attention to the great and wealthy, who are equally criminal, and less to be excused on the score of ignorance? By these marks the distinction is easily discovered between the mercenary self-seeker and the disinterested, zealous, and charitable Pastor: for the divine virtue of Charity, when genuine, ever calls forth the overflowings of benevolence and zeal equally in favour of the poor and the rich, and teaches us never to despair of the conversion of the most inveterate sinner, or to treat the most profligate and abandoned with harshness or contempt. The more I fathom and study the wonderful ways of Providence, the more cause shall I discover for exercising kindness and compassion towards unhappy sinners, and the more I shall be convinced, that severity is the fruit of a false zeal, and will tend rather to retard than advance their conversion. When I consider that Christ died for the salvation of all without exception, how do I know but the very man, whom I consider the most despicable and irreclaimable of all, may be a vessel of election, whose conversion wants nothing but the impulse of that external grace, which it might receive from my Charity? When I reflect that the extreme point of profligacy and vice is often the one at which grace chooses to begin its work, how can I doubt but that, to shew an unfortunate brother that, notwithstanding his disorders, I entertain hopes of his conversion, and accordingly to point out to him the resources of grace and mercy, are much more likely to soften his heart, to cover him with confusion, and to make him in love with virtue, than, by the absence of all Charity and tenderness in his regard, to give him to understand that I consider his case as hopeless?

CONCLUDING PRAYER.—Give me, O God, that *mild* and amiable Charity, which will make me, at all times, patient, kind, and condescending :—that *beneficent* Charity, by which I shall never be wearied in my efforts to do good :—and that *universal* Charity, which will cause me to extend my solicitude and zeal to all without exception—to those who resist my exhortation, as much as to the docile—to the poor, equally with the rich.— Whatever perfection I may arrive at in this heavenly virtue, I am sensible that I shall always remain far short of equalling the pattern which thou has shewn me in thy conversation with ignorant, obstinate, and carnal men during thy mortal life, and that my charge of the arduous duties of instructing, preaching, administering the sacraments, and trying to reclaim sinners, will not bear a comparison with thy labours in the same glorious works. But, my Saviour, I know that it is my duty, as it is now my earnest desire, to aim at an humble imitation of thy perfection! and, therefore, I now crave thy supporting grace to enable me to bear up under all the contradictions and trials of my ministry, with a meekness and Charity becoming a disciple of such a Master.

So far from having hitherto imitated thy meek, beneficent, and universal Charity, now that I come to compare my conduct with thine, I am confounded at the want of resemblance between us, and I cannot but fear, that the cause originates in a great deficiency of sincere love for thee, and of true zeal for thy honour and glory. But, oh, dear Jesus! I pray thee to deal with me in thy mercy, by repairing in me during these holy days of Retreat all that is defective. Enkindle in my breast those ardent flames, which will never let me grow weary in my duty, or think any exertion too great to bring even but one soul to thee. May I ever appear amongst my flock like a father who loves his children, and whose greatest delight is in their society; and may it never be my misfortune to alienate the affections and esteem of any by a misplaced asperity of language, or any treatment from which they might infer, that they possess no share in my Charity.

THIRD MEDITATION.

ON THE SUFFERINGS OF JESUS CHRIST IN HIS PASSION.

He was wounded for our iniquities, and bruised for our sins.—ISAIAS liii.

FIRST POINT.—The sufferings of Jesus Christ have at all times been a favourite subject of meditation with the saints, whose advancement in the virtues of a christian life ever kept pace with their increasing devotion to the great mystery of the Passion. By frequent and affectionate meditation on the sufferings of their divine Master, the martyrs acquired courage to brave the fury and torments of their persecutors, and by the same, have thousands of illustrious confessors and holy persons of every state learnt to die to themselves, to despise the empty and perishable goods of the world, and to attain to that eminence in virtue, which makes them the glory of the Spouse of Jesus Christ. So natural, indeed, is this devotion, that it is impossible to conceive a Christian to be a sincere lover of Jesus, and not to feel a strong impulse to be devout to his Passion, and frequently to attend at the foot of the cross to the heavenly lessons, which he teaches us from it.

Devotion, therefore, to the sufferings of our Redeemer is a duty incumbent upon every Christian, and particularly so on those, whose office is to form the hearts of others to piety and virtue. If Pastors neglect to study at the foot of the cross that sublime science which is nowhere else to be acquired, their language, however disguised by human eloquence, will be void of unction, and no better than a sounding brass, or a tinkling cymbal; and it is not to be doubted but that to their unacquaintance with this science, too many Pastors may justly attribute much of their want of success in their ministry.

The lesson, which above all others Jesus designed to inculcate in his Passion, is, how to behave under trials and afflictions. For this end he chose to endure more than ever fell to the lot of another human being. The effusion of a single drop of his sacred blood might have purchased our redemption; but had he refused to shed the last drop, and to submit to the unparalleled torments which were inflicted upon him, he would have left the great virtues of patience and resignation under sufferings and crosses but imperfectly illustrated. But, oh! when we kneel down before the image of our crucified Master, and cast our eyes upon that sacred body, all covered with wounds, leisurely contemplating the words which this expiring God addresses to us by the mouth of his prophet: *O all you, who pass by the way, attend and see, if there be sorrow like unto my sorrow* (Isaias i.), —when we look at that countenance all ghastly and disfigured with blows, that head crowned with thorns, that mouth drenched with gall, those hands and feet bored with nails, that side pierced with a lance, and those members all torn and dislocated,—what say our hearts at the sight of such a spectacle? Surely they tell us more forcibly than words can express, that we ought to be content to *carry in our bodies the mortification of Jesus Christ* (2 Cor. iv.). We feel convinced that an austere and mortified life is absolutely required of us,—that an aversion from suffering, the indulgence of our own ease, and the gratification of our senses, cannot possibly become disciples of such a Master. We learn that it is a duty to endeavour to overcome all the repugnances of nature, and to pay no attention to the pretexts which self-love so ingeniously suggests, for avoiding whatever is disagreeable to it—courageously to support the hardships attendant on our state of life—and cheerfully to perform all the painful and unpleasant functions of our ministry.

Had I the courage, under all my crosses

and afflictions, to fly to the foot of my crucifix, there to compare my sufferings with the pains and sorrows of my agonizing Saviour, how soon should I learn to endure them patiently, and what consolation should I derive from uniting them with those of my heavenly Master? And having once become familiar with the practice of these lessons, what facility would it afford of inculcating them to others? But, alas! instead of this, I am forced to acknowledge before God and to my own confusion, that, from my repugnance to every kind of suffering, I frequently yield to impatience under the ordinary trials incident to my state. I am obliged to confess that, for want of being perfectly familiar with the lessons taught in the school of my Saviour's Passion, I often indulge errors favourable to my own cowardice and sloth. I could not act thus—my sentiments and conduct would soon undergo a decided change, if the sufferings of Jesus Christ were well engraven upon my heart. However severe might be my crosses, they would all become, at least, supportable. On occasions when nature begins to repine, I should tell it, that its sufferings are nothing compared with those of Jesus Christ, and that it has not yet endured unto the shedding of blood. In short, I should be more feelingly convinced than I am, and should have less difficulty than I now have in convincing others, that the way of the cross is the high road to a crown, and that it is more desirable even to expire under it, than to live and die without penance.

SECOND POINT.—Another instructive consideration relative to our Saviour's Passion, is the motive for which he suffered. This was the glory of his Father and the salvation of men. He was perfectly at liberty either to suffer or not; but, his death being the condition on which man was to be saved and the injury done to his Father repaired, he felt too lively an interest both in one and the other, to refuse to make the voluntary sacrifice of his blood and his life; and he accordingly *became obedient unto death, even the death of the cross* (Phil. ii.).

Whatever were my condition in the fold of Christ, I should be obliged, like him, to practise continual mortification, for he has said to all his disciples, without exception: *whoever will come after me, let him deny himself and take up his cross daily* (Luke ix.). But, besides this general obligation contracted by all Christians, I have entered into a particular engagement, which I cannot violate without belying my profession, to lead a penitential life. My state is so essentially a state of penance, that it is impossible to discharge its functions, without encountering many trials, and renouncing the ordinary pleasures and comforts of life.

Having once made this solemn engagement, it is no longer in my power to retrace my steps; and all the choice which remains for me is, to derive merit or demerit from my trials, according to the manner in which I bear them.

Those who cheerfully and affectionately embrace the cross, find it far more sweet and delightful than the most refined enjoyments are to the slaves of sensual pleasure. But the Christian, who takes it up with reluctance, or who attempts to throw off any part of the yoke by studying his own ease, forfeits much of the merit, and all the consolation, of the cross.—How highly, then, ought I to esteem the happy necessity, which furnishes me with the means of taking part in the sufferings of the Son of God, of giving glory to the Almighty, and of making satisfaction for my sins. Oh! it ought to be a source of the greatest comfort to me to know, that my life of daily and constant penance was marked out for me by God himself, and that he called me to it, by calling me to the sacred ministry. How ought I to praise and bless his infinite goodness!

THIRD POINT.—If I consider the manner in which Jesus suffered, I shall find it to have been with the most invincible patience and unalterable constancy. He was *like a lamb in the hands of the shearer*, making no resistance; or *as a sheep led to the slaughter*, *not opening his mouth.* How admirable was his silence when Pilate pronounced the sentence of his condemnation! When the insulting rabble dragged him bound with cords into the city—when the soldiers tore his flesh with whips in the pretor's hall, and placed a crown of thorns upon his head—when the executioners pierced his hands and feet with nails and fastened him to the cross—not a murmur of impatience escaped his lips. So perfect was his patience, that it might have been doubted whether he was was not insensible to pain. But I know that he really suffered, and likewise, that he has enabled thousands of others to endure with serenity sufferings little less intense than his own. It is not probable that my patience will ever be put to so severe a test; but a true spirit of mortification will teach me, at least, not to repine under the ordinary visitations of Providence.

Possessed of this spirit of patience and mortification, I shall not be morose and fretful under every trifling infirmity that befalls me, nor treat myself with such studied indulgence and compassion. I shall not murmur at every little privation, and be angry on occasion of a slight want of attention from those about me. To these and even greater crosses I shall submit in silence; or, if I speak, so far from complaining, I shall rejoice with St. Paul, in being clothed with the mortification of Jesus. These ought to be my sentiments, this my language, in the times of infirmity and sickness; and if they be not such, the only cause which can be assigned is, that I am a stranger to those lessons, which my Saviour has inculcated in his Passion.

An essential character of evangelical mortification and patience, is constancy and perseverance. The sufferings of the Son of God, and his patience endurance of them, continued without interruption to the moment when he breathed his last upon the cross.— He consummated his sacrifice with constancy, and death alone put an end to his pains. In like manner, it will not suffice for me to mortify myself occasionally, and suffer with patience only for a time; I must carry my cross daily, and submit to whatever sufferings Providence may please to send me at all times and under all circumstances; and I must persevere in this holy disposition unto the end.

It is related of one of the saints, that on his death-bed he acknowledged having treated his body with too much severity. Alas! is it not my daily misfortune to err in the opposite extreme? An occasional effort to subdue my senses by refusing to them what they crave, would seem to confer a right to take an early opportunity of weakly condescending to their demands. The slightest inconvenience is a pretext for omitting my penitential exercises, and a sufficient motive for granting myself indulgences, with which a good will would easily teach me to dispense. The farther I advance in years, the more I persuade myself that I am entitled to study my own ease, as if I could ever cease to be bound by the laws of the Gospel of Jesus Christ. It is true, with reference to age and constitution, that prudence is to be observed in the use of corporal austerities. But even this prudence should be confined within certain limits, and not carried to excess—a fault, which would easily be corrected, were I truly sensible of the advantage of living in penance, and of expiring, like Jesus Christ, in the arms of the cross.

CONCLUDING PRAYER.—O Saviour of the world! since thou hast redeemed me by the cross, how can I hope to arrive at eternal life, but by the way of the cross? and were it possible, how could I desire it? In becoming my Saviour, thou did also become my guide in the path of salvation; and, consequently, I can have no just pretensions to the happiness which thou has merited for me, but by following thee in the way which thou hast marked out, which is the way of the cross. Can I contemplate thy sacred and innocent body all torn with stripes and covered with wounds, and still be willing to pamper my own criminal flesh and treat it with indulgence? Can I see thy thirst quenched with vinegar, and thy palate embittered with gall, and yet seek to gratify all my appetites, and complain when I cannot procure them every thing that they desire? Can I behold thee expiring under the most excruciating agony, and yet not be content to pass my days otherwise than in self-indulgence and ease?

Ah! dear Lord! I know that the slave has no right to expect better treatment than his master. Dedicated as I am to thee by the strongest possible engagements, and elevated to the sublime dignity of being made a pillar in thy Church, what shall I be able to answer at thy tribunal, when thou shalt point out to me the wide difference between thyself and me? Even at present, how can I avoid being covered with confusion, when I look at thee and thy cross? Oh! this alone should excite in me a spirit of mortification and penance;—it should clothe me with new courage, and strengthen me against the most violent assaults of my senses and corrupt nature. Henceforth, at least, my dear Jesus, my sole ambition shall be, like that of thy apostle, to know nothing but thee, and thee crucified. But let me not possess this knowledge in speculation only; enable me to reduce it to practice. Let me not be content to contemplate thee upon the cross; but teach me also by thy grace to carry my cross after thee, and to carry it well; for this, I know, is sanctity itself, and the summit of perfection.

CONSIDERATION.

ON READING AND STUDY.

FIRST POINT.—Placed in the Church for the instruction and edification of the faithful, Pastors are obliged to expound the mysteries of religion, to develope the maxims of Christian morality, to explain the worship and ceremonies of the Church, and to be, at all times, ready to meet with strong and invincible answers the objections of incredulity and error. Hence it has ever been the spirit of the Church, to require in those, to whom she confides the pastoral charge, learning adequate to these arduous and important duties; and never, since the foundation of Christianity, was there greater need of wise and enlightened Pastors, of men prepared *to give an account of the hope that is in them* (1 Pet. iii.), able to repel the attacks of ridicule and calumny, and qualified to expose the sophistry of the enemies of religion, than in these unhappy days, when infidelity is so successfully following up the attempts of heresy to undermine religion, and to tarnish the beauty of the sacred dogmas of Jesus

Christ.—The direction of the faithful in the tribunal of penance is another office, which demands no small degree of learning. So wide is the range of Christian morality, and so complicated are frequently the cases connected with it, that the want of a competent knowledge of practical theology renders a person unfit even to enter the sanctuary, and much more so to have the charge of souls. A priest cannot sit in the sacred chair without being obliged to exercise his judgment upon the divine law; and for the decisions which he makes respecting it he becomes responsible to its Author. The lowest degree of knowledge, which he can be allowed to bring to this awful duty, is such an acquaintance with general principles and their consequences as will qualify him to discern difficulties where they exist, and to doubt upon points which he cannot immediately decide.

These considerations are sufficient to convince me of the necessity of continual application to Reading and Study. To think myself so well versed in the divine law, as to be under no further obligation of applying to it, would be an evident proof that I am wise only in my own conceit. Nay, whatever knowledge I may at present possess, it is certain that it can be retained only by persevering Study and application—that, if I neglect these, many subjects, on which my ideas are at present sufficiently clear and distinct, will soon become involved in obscurity. Hence, if I neglect Reading and Study, I have no security against the faults and errors, which are so apt to glide into the exercise of my sacred functions; for to calculate upon the assistance and direction of the Holy Spirit, without using my own exertions, would be but a blind presumption. However numerous may be my external occupations, surely I can want no further inducement than this to spend in Study the intervals of leisure which I can command; and if my public duties leave much of my time unemployed, it must either be given to Study, or spent far less profitably. Have I hitherto been sensible of my duty in this respect? and have I practised it? If not, I must reform without delay, and immediately begin to apply myself to a course of useful Study.

SECOND POINT.—A priest or Pastor of souls can never be at a loss for proper subjects of application. His difficulty will rather be, amongst so many to select the most necessary and useful. Taking, however, for his rule the maxims and examples of the brightest ornaments of the Church, and the most successful labourers in the vineyard of the Lord, the Holy Scriptures will be a leading object of his pursuit. Knowing that the great and good have ever found them to be an inexhaustible fund of exhortation, and have derived from them their most solid instruction, the zealous Pastor will try literally to fulfil the divine injunction to *meditate upon them sitting in his house and going abroad, lying down to rest, and rising up.* (Deut. vi.)— The historical books of the Old Testament will furnish him with copious materials for illustrating the mercy, the justice, and the other attributes of the Deity, for enforcing all the moral virtues, and even silencing the voice of incredulity itself. The writings of the Prophets will unfold to him some of the strongest arguments in support of the Church of Christ, besides abounding with a sublimity of sentiment and fire of expression, with which the finest productions of profane literature will bear no comparison. A tolerable acquaintance with the sense of the Psalms, which constitute so large a portion of his daily prayer, will be a considerable help to his private devotion; and the books of Wisdom will furnish maxims applicable to every circumstance and state of life. But the writings of the Evangelists, and the other books of the New Testament, will be his daily bread; and in the profound meditation upon the Gospels, and on the Epistles of the Great Apostle, he will become familiar with that celestial science, which is so superior to all the *persuasive words of human wisdom* (1 Cor. ii).

A Pastor's next care will be, to keep up a

thorough acquaintance with all the dogmas of faith and the terms used by the Church in delivering them, drawing in his mind clear and distinct lines between points which are strictly of faith, mere matters of theological opinion, and false or heretical doctrine.— Without this he cannot possibly be prepared, either to explain the Christian doctrine, or to fortify his people with clear and forcible arguments against heretics, infidels, and all who oppugn the truth.

Then, as to moral theology and books of piety and devotion, so large is the field which these open to the pursuits of a Pastor, that all the time he can possibly devote to them will be little enough to make him perfect in the art, which it should be the summit of his ambition to acquire—that of directing souls and conducting them to God. Upon his assiduity in these Studies depend, in a great degree, his own advancement in virtue, and the right performance of two of his most important functions, the Ministry of the Word of God, and the administration of the sacrament of reconciliation. It is, indeed, a difficult task to acquire the art of directing souls —to learn the human heart—to become a good judge of the interior dispositions of those, who present themselves at the sacred tribunal—to suggest the sentiments of repentance best adapted to the different dispositions of penitents—to correct habitual sinners—to soften the hardened—to spur on the slothful—to encourage the pusillanimous—and to put all in the way of arriving at that perfection which God requires of them.

I see plainly that the knowledge requisite for the perfect discharge of the duties of the ministry is immense, and, consequently, I am convinced that, if I design to save my soul, I cannot with a safe conscience employ my leisure hours in the indulgence of my own ease, but am obliged to apply myself to sacred Studies. Were my sentiments other than these, it would be an undoubted proof that I feel not the responsibility attached to my ministry, and that I am blind to its difficulties and dangers.

Third Point.—Few Pastors, who are really attentive to the spiritual necessities of the faithful under their care, assiduous in the administration of the sacraments, zealous in reclaiming sinners, in preaching, exhorting and instructing, and earnestly devoted to the Studies appertaining to their vocation, will find much time to spare for the acquirement or improvement of those accomplishments which profane literature or amusing books are thought to confer; and it can scarcely be questioned but an indifference to such pursuits would be greatly in favour of the true interests of religion, and would remove no unfrequent obstacle to the attainment of perfection. Still, it might be regarded as a doctrine bordering upon excessive rigour to assert, that these Studies, when used only for recreation, and not suffered to encroach upon the time necessary for higher pursuits, are altogether unlawful. Those, however, who, through motives of religion, and with a view to their greater santification, deny themselves this indulgence, will undoubtedly find their self-denial amply repaid by the facility which it will afford for perfecting themselves in internal recollection, and every other branch of genuine piety.—For such Studies have necessarily a great tendency to divide the heart, to distract the mind, and to nourish vanity; and, from an innocent amusement or recreation, they are too apt to degenerate into a sinful passion. The most lenient inference to be drawn from these observations is, that a priest cannot be too guarded in' the degree of indulgence, which he allows himself in profane Studies; for, if the fascination of human wisdom once gain the ascendency in his heart, his piety and fervour will daily and very sensibly be diminished; his office will be recited with hurry, and his meditations abridged; and he will be led either into the total omission of many points of his duty, or to perform them in a careless manner.

What precautions have I hitherto taken against the dangers to which I am exposed in this respect? Have I been careful, not to give too much of my vacant time to profane Reading, and not to make that my daily and habitual employment, to which a few short moments are all that I should allow? Have I not suffered my relish for it to grow into a passion, to the indulgence of which I scarcely set any bounds? Have I not been so fascinated with the pleasure of light and amusing books, as to neglect some part of my sacred functions, or, at least, to hurry them over, through eagerness to resume my favourite pursuit? Have I not so far feasted my imagination with some branch of profane Study, as to become disgusted with spiritual books, *preferring*, as the apostle words it, *frivolous discourses to sound doctrine and fables to the truth?*

Another, and not the least, material question, which I ought to ask my heart is, whether I have not made my acquirements in profane literature, and my knowledge of books, subservient to ostentation and vanity, and substituted these as a means of gaining esteem and admiration, in the place of that sublime science, which alone can really advance the glory of God and the true interests of religion—the knowledge of Christ crucified? I may be assured that the books, which I peruse with so much eagerness and relish, will not teach me the science of salvation, and that without this, every other science is but vanity.

CONCLUDING MEDITATION.

THE RESURRECTION OF JESUS CHRIST THE MODEL OF A NEW LIFE.

As Christ arose from the dead, so we must walk in the newness of life.—ROM. vi.

FIRST POINT.—That divine and miraculous power, which, during the days of his mortality, the Son of God had exercised in so many ways, and displayed on so many occasions, was still more wonderfully manifested in his Resurrection to a new and immortal existence. At the appointed moment his lifeless corpse instantly became reanimated by the return of his blessed soul and divinity, when, bursting open the monument, he arose from the bosom of the earth. Well does the Church apply to this splendid victory over death, the words adopted by St. Paul from the Prophet Osee: *O death, where is thy victory? O death, where is thy sting?* (1 Cor. xv.)—words, which give me to understand by what virtue this miracle of the Resurrection was wrought, and show how death, though permitted to exercise a limited dominion over him, was still obliged to yield to his omnipotence.

The Resurrection of Jesus Christ is designed

to be the model of my spiritual Resurrection to a new life; though it would be a gross error, and the height of presumption in me, to suppose myself capable, like him, of arising by my own strength. I am the essence of weakness and dependence. Of myself, then, it were vain to hope to conquer my evil habits, and to divest myself of my manifold imperfections. In this respect, therefore, it is certain, that I cannot imitate Jesus Christ, who arose from the grave by the simple exercise of his own will. But, supposing the assistance of divine grace, which is ever at hand, and of which I have been made sensible during these days of retirement, it is equally certain that, by co-operating with it and following its guidance, I may complete the work of my spiritual Resurrection and sanctification.

As Jesus, in rising again, had to divest his body of the winding sheet, in which it was involved, so must I disengage myself from the dominion of my natural inclinations and passions. The huge stone closing the entrance of the monument had to be rolled away. In like manner, the life of habitual sloth and self-indulgence, which I have hitherto led, is a weight, which must be removed, before I can rise to the newness of life. He overcame the guard stationed by his enemies around his tomb. Besides the invisible enemies of my perfection and salvation, who are instigated by malice to hold me in perpetual bondage, I have many other enemies that must be combated and conquered, before I can hope to imitate the Resurrection of Jesus Christ. For this end, I must lay aside all human respect—I must disregard the remarks of men—I must not be influenced by the custom and the example of others—I must sever myself from every tie of friendship, which divides my heart, and renounce every engagement or occupation, that interferes with the strict and faithful discharge of my sacred duties;—in a word, I must forsake everything, which, during my Retreat, I have discovered to have been hitherto an impediment to my attaining the perfection of my state.—Jesus had promised his disciples, that on the third day after his death and burial, he would rise again. In the fulfilment of this promise, he surmounted all difficulties and obstacles. During these days of Retirement, which I am now bringing to a close, I have purposed and resolved many things: I have over and over again protested to the Almighty, that I will in future change my life and conduct in such and such particulars. The time is now coming, when I am to give proof of my sincerity by my fidelity to these engagements, and by beginning without delay to put in practice all that I have resolved. My conduct will soon shew whether or not I am sincere. Ah! my God, let not my resolutions fail, and my courage give way in the hour of trial. I know thy grace will not be wanting; and woe to me, if I relapse through my own fault.

SECOND POINT.—Jesus Christ, at his Resurrection, took a new life, a life glorious and altogether different from his mortal one.— This God and Saviour, heretofore subject to all the miseries incident to his poor and lowly condition, and to the pain and ignominy of a life of suffering, in his re-appearance was clothed with light, so that the glory of his body surpassed the splendour of the sun. In his first life, his body was weak, sensitive, and liable to the infirmities of human nature; but, in his second, it was endowed with superhuman strength, and was incapable of suffering. Its glory was dazzling to the sight; by its agility it could transport itself instantly from place to place; and by its subtlety it resembled a spirit, to which nothing material could oppose the least resistance. Hence it may be said, that the effect of this mystery was a permanent transfiguration of his body far more resplendent than that witnessed by the favoured Apostles on Mount Thabor.

If I design my Resurrection to be real, and to be marked by the perfection, which ought to distinguish my future from my past life, I must undergo a transformation accompanied by characters similar to those of the new life of Jesus Christ. Both in my interior and exterior life there is much that requires to be reformed and renewed. My interior demands my first attention. On returning to my ordinary occupations, the assumption of an air of greater gravity than heretofore, and a show of external deportment more consistent with the sacerdotal character, would suffice to preserve outward appearances; but to what would all this amount if my heart be allowed to continue always the same? The principal work before me, then, is to rectify my motives and intentions, to restrain the swellings of pride, and to divest myself of indolence and sloth. I must undeceive myself respecting the false notions and errors with which I have been impressed: I must disengage my heart from every attachment to things or persons, however harmless it may appear in itself, which is not in God and for God. I must cast off that self-love, to which I have now discovered myself to have been the slave; and, in a word, my interior must be entirely renewed.

The natural and necessary result of this renewal of my heart will be a total change in my external deportment. Bearing constantly in mind the duties which I owe to God, to my neighbour, and to myself, I shall be stimulated to discharge them with fidelity.— The disedification, which my past sloth may have given, will be repaired by the edification that my flock will derive from witnessing my exactness and zeal. But, my God, what am I saying? Is this really the happy change that is now wrought in me? Alas! I know that, during these moments of fervour, and in the warmth of heavenly meditation, such sentiments as now animate my breast are easily adopted. But, I know also, that to reduce them to practice is not the work of simple meditation, nor even of a few days passed in silence and Retreat. Still this Retreat must be an excellent foundation of future good; and it cannot be an unimportant point that I am going to leave my solitude in good dispositions, and fortified with holy resolutions of leading a new life. The former it shall be my constant study to retain, and the latter I will renew from day to day. By these means, and through the help of thy supporting grace, I hope to persevere.

THIRD POINT.—How imperfect would have been the Resurrection of Jesus Christ, had he not, in resuming life, clothed himself also with immortality. But *Christ*, says St. Paul, *rising from the dead dieth now no more, death shall no more have dominion over him* (Rom. vi.). This prediction has for many ages been verified, and it will continue to be so for ages without end. What a contrast is there between the Resurrection of Jesus Christ, and that of those who, when this God-Man expired on the cross, were permitted to arise for a time from their monuments, but were soon again consigned to the sleep of death. This *First-born among the dead* forsook the silent tomb never more to return to it.

Blessed life of immortality, which represents to me one of the most necessary virtues at which I ought to aim, but which, unhappily, is rarely attained—that of perseverance! Few there are who do not for some days, and even weeks, profit by a Retreat. Not confining themselves to mere words and sentiments, they proceed to action, and enter with seeming alacrity on the performance of their good resolutions. But alas! in too many cases this Resurrection is only of short duration, and they fall from their holy purposes. It does not belong to me to judge other individuals; but is not this the true history of my own misfortunes? Where is the fruit of my former Retreats? How long did I persevere in the fervent dispositions, which I then conceived? And what difference is there between my present and former dispositions? Perhaps, even, it would be better for me, were I, at this moment, in the state I was in at some former period of my life. It certainly would, if, instead of advancing, I have been growing less fervent and zealous from year to year.

Be this, however, as it may, it is certain

N

that Almighty God has frequently enlightened me with a sense of my duty, and moved my heart with a desire to practise it. Often, in the sincerity of my repentance and in the fervour of prayer, have I said to him in my heart, like David: *now I begin* (Ps. lxxvi.). Alas! I have said, and have begun; but I have not persevered. I have been led by the weight of corrupt nature into my former ways of neglect and sloth. And shall this Retreat be followed by the same lamentable consequences? At the present moment, I feel in good dispositions; but, how long will they continue? On what can I ground a rational hope of more constancy and longer perseverance than heretofore?

It is well for me that, although my will be naturally changeable and inconstant, religion furnishes me with the means of rendering it immoveable. These I must for the future carefully employ. Having discovered by self-examination the true cause of my former relapses, I must study to remove it. Have I not placed more reliance on the strength of my resolutions, than on the supporting arm of him, who alone can give perseverance? Were not my resolutions made in mere general terms, without descending minutely to the particular duties, which religion and my state of life impose upon me? To form a correct judgment on these points, I can take no safer rule than to examine, how I practised these various duties. Was I, then, exact and fervent in the exercise of prayer? Was I accustomed to make my daily meditation? Did I carefully examine my conscience every night? Had I frequent recourse, with due preparation, to the sacrament of penance? Was my daily approach to the altar preceded, accompanied, and followed by the devotion which is due to the tremendous mysteries? Was I careful to recite my office with respect, attention, and devotion? If, after having diligently and fervently gone through the exercise of a Retreat, I did not persevere, it must be attributable to a neglect of some one or more of these necessary means. Hence it follows, that, if I would not again incur the same misfortune, I must in future pursue a different conduct. Alas! had I not, during the past years, been so studious of my own ease, to the prejudice of the essential duties of a Christian life, instead of now discovering nothing but motives of regret for the past, I might be living in the enjoyment of true interior peace, as the fruit of past labours and combats. It is, however, time that I should now, once for all, take a decided step, by entering diligently upon, and continuing in, the fervent practice of the means of perseverance unto the end. My years are rolling on in quick succession, and it may be, that they are bordering upon their close. My only security is to give all that remain to God.

SIXTH DAY.

CONCLUDING PRAYER.—O Almighty God, now that the Retreat, to which in thy mercy thou hast been pleased to call me, is on the point of being brought to a conclusion, my last, but most fervent supplication, is, that thou wilt vouchsafe to put the finishing stroke to thy own victory. Stretch forth thy hand to raise me perfectly from the slothful state in which I have hitherto lived. Enable me thoroughly to subdue my imperfections and evil habits: repress the power of my spiritual enemies: in the discharge of my arduous duties render me proof against the influence of human respect, and evil customs and example, that, having nothing in view but thee and thy holy law, I may be indifferent to all that the world can either give or take away. Let no difficulties discourage me, and let my future behaviour shew, that these happy days of retirement have not been spent in vain. Being now, as I trust, truly risen again, let my newness of life henceforth proclaim the triumph of thy holy grace.

O Lord, when I look at myself, my own natural weakness, of which I never can divest myself, greatly alarms me. Corrupt nature of itself necessarily tends to evil, and, however good may be my present sentiments and dispositions, past experience convinces me, that no dependence can be placed on them. But thou, O God, hast taught me, ever to expect thy aid in the hour of danger and temptation, provided I have earnest recourse to thee, with an entire distrust in myself and an humble confidence in thy power and goodness. In these dispositions, O tender and Almighty Father, I pray that I may never more be so unfortunate as to yield to the influence of my frail and sinful nature. Let thy grace distinguish my future from my past life. Give me, Oh! give me, the grace of perseverance.

In asking for this singular blessing of perseverance, I pray thee, also, to strengthen me in the use of the only means whereby it can be secured. Make me henceforth regular and earnest in the holy exercises of prayer and meditation: enable me always to say the divine office with respect, attention, and devotion: give me such a veneration for the mysteries of the Altar as will cause me to study daily to celebrate them with an increase of fervour and love: strengthen me to discharge the functions of thy ministry with exactness, zeal and charity; and let me, at all times, keep that strict watch over my interior dispositions and external conduct, which will induce me to take the alarm at the most distant symptoms of returning sloth.

O heavenly Father! thou knowest the number of my days: but, whether they are to be few or many, I wish to give them all to thee, as well in reparation of the past, as to secure at the hour of my departure hence one of those glorious crowns, which in the mansions of eternity will distinguish thy faithful ministers from the rest of thy elect. Once more, then, my God, I say to thee, and I trust it is with greater sincerity than I have ever yet said it: *Now I begin; let this be the change of thy right hand.*

O glorious Virgin Mary, Mother of Jesus, and special Patroness of Pastors of souls! my holy patrons, N. and N. and all ye blessed citizens of the heavenly Jerusalem! recommend, I conjure you, these my resolutions and supplications at the throne of grace, that, through your intercession, they may be more favourably received. Pray for me, that, from this day forward, I may never more cease to live as becomes a true and faithful minister of Jesus Christ, and, at the hour of my death, may be united to your happy society for ages without end.

FINIS.

CONTENTS.

	PAGE.
Meditation for the Eve of a Retreat	1

FIRST DAY.

First Meditation.—On the Perfection required in a Pastor	6
Second Meditation.—On Mortal Sin	13
Third Meditation.—On Venial Sin	20
Consideration.—On the Perfection of our Ordinary Actions	27

SECOND DAY.

First Meditation.—On Scandal and Good Example	34
Second Meditation.—On Spiritual Sloth	41
Third Meditation.—On the Abuse of Grace	48
Consideration.—On Mental Prayer	55

THIRD DAY.

First Meditation.—On the Loss of Time	63
Second Meditation.—On Death	69
Third Meditation.—On Judgment	76
Consideration.—On the Prayers of a Pastor for his Flock, and particularly on the Divine Office	87

Fourth Day.

First Meditation.—On Hell 95
Second Meditation.—On the Parable of the Prodigal Son 104
Third Meditation.—On the Reign of Jesus Christ in the Soul of a Pastor 114
Consideration.—On the Sacrifice of the Mass 123

Fifth Day.

First Meditation.—On the Humility of Jesus Christ in his Incarnation 131
Second Meditation.—On the Poverty of Jesus Christ in his Birth 140
Third Meditation.—On the Obedience of Jesus Christ in his Flight into Egypt 149
Consideration.—On Conversation with our Neighbour 159

Sixth Day.

First Meditation.—On the Hidden Life of Jesus Christ 167
Second Meditation.—On the Charity of Jesus Christ in his Active Life 175
Third Meditation.—On the Sufferings of Jesus Christ in his Passion 185
Consideration.—On Reading and Study 195
Concluding Meditation.—The Resurrection of Jesus Christ the Model of a New Life 203